Editor: John Morton
Designer: Vivienne Gordon
Picture Researcher: Caroline Mitchell
Artwork: Paul Sullivan

The editor and author would like to thank the following who gave their kind cooperation in helping to illustrate this book:
R. Hickman, Libritz Stamps, Apsley, Herts
Stanley Gibbons Auctions, London WC2
Stanley Gibbons Ltd, London WC2
Stanley Gibbons Publications Ltd, Ringwood, Hants
Vera Trinder Ltd, London WC2
The photograph of the Tyrian Plum stamps on page 28 is reproduced by gracious permission of Her Majesty The Queen.

Other photographs reproduced courtesy of:
The British Library
Harmers of London
Hulton-Deutsch Collection
B.R. Lewis (Mrs.)
H.R. Lewis
Mansell Collection
The Mary Evans Picture Library
R. Mewse
J. Morton
T. Newman and R. Shelley
W. Payne
The Philatelic Traders' Society
The Post Office
Barrie Smith, French Picture Library
R. Topley

Text and design copyright © 1990 by Simon & Schuster Young Books
Photographs copyright © 1990 by Martyn Chillmaid

Library of Congress Cataloging-in-Publication Data

Lewis, Brenda Ralph.
    Stamps!: a young collector's guide/Brenda Ralph Lewis. —1st
American ed.
        p.   cm.
    "Originally published in Great Britain in 1990 by Simon and Schuster Young Books"—T.p. verso.
    Includes index.
    Summary: Introduces readers to the history and great variety of postage stamps and examines some of the techniques used in identifying and collecting them.
    ISBN 0-525-67341-5
    1. Postage-stamps—Collectors and collecting—Juvenile literature.
[1. Postage stamps—Collectors and collecting.]   I. Title.
HE6213.L48   1991
769.56—dc20   90-6522
                          93-83   CIP
                                                                          AC

First published in the United States in 1991 by Lodestar Books, an affiliate of Dutton Children's Books, a division of Penguin Books USA Inc.

Published simultaneously in Canada by McClelland & Stewart, Toronto

Originally published in Great Britain in 1990 by Simon and Schuster Young Books, Simon and Schuster Ltd., Wolsey House, Wolsey Road, Hemel Hempstead, Hertfordshire, HP2 4SS England

Printed in Great Britain   ISBN: 0-525-67341-5
First American Edition   10 9 8 7 6 5 4 3 2 1

Stamps!

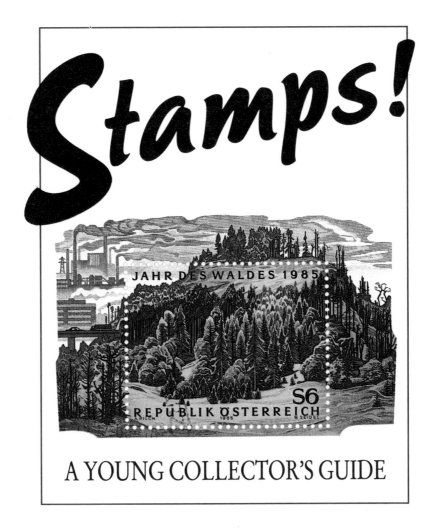

A YOUNG COLLECTOR'S GUIDE

Brenda Ralph Lewis

LODESTAR BOOKS

DUTTON   NEW YORK

CONTENTS

INTRODUCTION	**6**
BEFORE STAMPS WERE INVENTED	**8**
THE FIRST STAMPS	**10**
THE FIRST COLLECTORS	**12**
WHAT SHALL I COLLECT? All the world or one country?	**14**
WHAT SHALL I COLLECT? Thematics	**16**
WHAT SHALL I COLLECT? Themes in themes	**18**
STORIES IN STAMPS	**20**
MINT OR USED?	**22**
WHAT STAMPS TELL YOU	**24**
STRANGE STAMP STORIES	**26**
FAMOUS COLLECTORS	**28**
STAMP ALPHABETS	**30**
PHILATELICALLY TERMINATED	**32**
WHY STAMPS ARE ISSUED	**34**
HOW STAMPS ARE MADE 1 From paintbrush to post office	**36**
HOW STAMPS ARE MADE 2 Different ways to print stamps	**38**
STAMPS SEEN IN DIFFERENT WAYS	**40**
STRANGE STAMPS	**42**
COLLECTING COVERS	**44**
FAMOUS FORGERS	**46**
STAMP SHOPS AND FAIRS	**48**

BUYING STAMPS BY MAIL	50
CLUBS AND EXHIBITIONS	52
CATALOGS	54
FAMOUS STAMPS	56
AIRMAILS	58
ODD MAILS	60
STAMPS GO TO WAR	62
STAMPS WITH MESSAGES	64
THE TOOLS OF COLLECTING	66
HOW TO CARE FOR YOUR STAMPS	68
HOW TO ARRANGE STAMPS	70
STAMP OMNIBUSES	72
STAMP ERRORS	74
THE BEAUTY OF STAMPS	76
POSTMARKS	78
CINDERELLAS Stamps that are not stamps	80
STAMP FINDER	82
STAMP MAPS	84
GLOSSARY	88
PARTS OF A STAMP	92
FINDING OUT MORE	93
INDEX	94

INTRODUCTION

You could say a stamp is just a piece of paper with gum on the back and a picture on the front. You could also say that it exists just to pay for postage through the mails. You would be perfectly right to say all this.

But there's much more to stamps than that! Otherwise, no one would bother to collect them, write books about them or pay huge prices for rare ones.

For a start, stamps are often richly-colored miniature works of art. Their fascinating designs can show you sports, flowers and other plants, every animal you can think of, art, transportation old and new and, in fact, almost whatever interests you.

There are millions of stamps from scores of countries on hundreds of subjects. So you'll never run out of stamps to choose from when you're looking for something interesting to collect. This book tells you about the many different types of stamps and how to collect them. You'll learn where to buy them and how to take care of them. Most of the stamps shown in this book have been enlarged and printed bigger than they really are so you can see them clearly.

Use the index to find subjects and stamps quickly. The glossary at the end of the book explains the most important words and terms you'll come across in stamp collecting. The glossary also has an enlarged picture that shows all the different parts of a stamp. Next to the glossary is a "Stamp Finder" to help you identify strange stamps and discover where they come from.

As you'll soon see, stamp collecting, or philately, is an exciting world of discovery and adventure. But be warned. If you read this book, you may be bitten by a dangerous bug—the stamp bug! Once bitten, you may never be the same again!

▽ This is what stamps used in Afghanistan looked like about a hundred years ago. Stamps like this are called "primitives." One reason for this is that they are roughly printed and look homemade. Many other very early stamps are also primitives.

△ The glowing butterfly on this 1984 stamp of Hong Kong is from a set of stamps showing traditional Chinese lanterns. Millions of Chinese people live in Hong Kong, so it is not surprising that the colony's stamps often illustrate Chinese traditions and customs.

▷ The first three stamps of India—the Scinde Dawk issues—were very unusual. Made in Britain in 1852, they were embossed on wax discs. This half anna scarlet Scinde Dawk was made of sealing wax. Scinde, now in Pakistan, was then a province of British-ruled India.

◁ There is a printing error in one of these two British stamps. They come from a 1975 set about cycling. Can you spot the error?

Answer : The head at the top right is in the proper place on the top stamp. In the bottom stamp, though, the head has dropped down.

△ Thematic stamps show a particular theme or subject. There are thousands of thematics on hundreds of different subjects, including cars, birds or flags, so you can collect whatever interests you. This Italian stamp is a geography thematic showing beautiful countryside at Ravello.

▽ Collecting stamps tells you a great deal about how the Post Office works. The U.S. strip of stamps shows postal workers doing the many different jobs needed to deliver a letter to you.

A zip code for your address speeds up the delivery of letters. This is the message behind the red Dutch stamp of 1978, when zip codes were first used in the Netherlands.

BEFORE STAMPS WERE INVENTED

Postal services, or collecting and delivering letters, packets and parcels, are very much older than postage stamps. There were postal services in China six thousand years ago, and Egypt about a thousand years later. These very early mail services were used mainly by kings and queens, royal officials and merchants. However, their letters were not like ours but were written on baked clay tablets carried in clay "envelopes."

Later on, letters carried all over the Roman Empire by the *Cursus Publicus*, the Roman Post Office, were written on wax tablets, thin pieces of wood or animal skins. Paper was not used for letters until over two thousand years ago, when it was invented in China. The use of paper later spread to Europe.

Letters and other postal items were carried by special messengers, the first mailmen. Some traveled on foot, others on horseback. The *tabellarii*, the Roman letter carriers, often used carts.

When letter carriers came to a town, they would ring a bell or blow loudly on post horns to tell people that their mail was arriving. The first post horn was probably used by the Butchers' Guild in Germany in the twelfth century. (A guild was a group of craftworkers, like goldsmiths, weavers or bakers, who followed the same trade.) Many mail services at that time and for a long time afterwards were run by trade guilds so that their members could communicate with one another. Before a German butcher could join the guild he not only had to own a horse, but also had to promise to deliver the guild's letters.

△ This 1976 Italian stamp is from a set that tells the story of the mail from ancient to modern times. This stamp, the first in the set, illustrates a cart used by the postal service of Ancient Rome, the *Cursus Publicus*.

▽ In ancient Peru, high up in the Andes Mountains of South America, *chasquis*, or messengers, used to run along the mountain roads, delivering messages for the *Sapa Inca*, the emperor. Spain conquered Peru in the 1540s, and this Spanish stamp shows a *chasquis* blowing panpipes to warn people he was coming.

▷ This is what European mailmen looked like five or six hundred years ago. The mailman on this French stamp was a royal messenger who carried letters for the king and the royal court.

▷ This 1988 Finnish stamp, issued on the 350th anniversary of Finland's Post Office, shows a postal tariff. It lists the cost of sending letters to different nearby towns, such as Oslo or Stockholm. It also gives prices for heavier letters or parcels. The heavier the letter and the further the distance, the higher the price.

▷ On the tiny Atlantic island of Ascension, three hundred years ago, letters to or from the rest of the world were left in bottles on a rock out at sea. This was because it was too dangerous for sailing ships to come right up to the rocky island. Rowing boats brought letters from the rock to the island or to a waiting sailing ship. This 1980 Ascension stamp shows bottles awaiting collection.

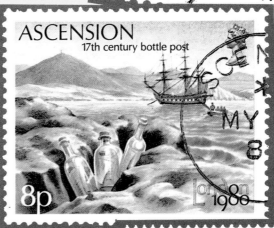

◁ Several countries have put post horns on their stamps as a reminder of the days when letter carriers blew horns to tell people that letters were arriving. This definitive stamp from Norway is one of these stamps. Austria, Germany and Switzerland are among other countries that have put post horns on their stamps.

◁ Letter carriers sometimes rang bells instead of blowing post horns to tell people the mail had arrived. This British stamp shows a letter carrier with his bell in 1839. Do you think the letter in his left hand had a prepaid adhesive stamp on the envelope?

△ Mail coaches faced many dangers. Bad roads, filled with potholes, were almost impassable in bad weather, and coaches often got stuck in the mud. Highwaymen might steal the mail or the passengers' valuables. This British stamp shows a coach in a storm.

THE FIRST STAMPS

In 1840 the Post Office in Great Britain was in trouble. It was losing money. This was mostly because of the way it charged people for carrying letters. The greater the distance a letter had to go, the greater the price the Post Office charged. A letter also cost more if it was very heavy or contained more than one sheet of paper. Postage was paid not by the sender of a letter, but by the person who received it. If that person did not want to pay the postage, he or she just refused to accept the letter. Some people put short messages on the envelope which told the person they had written to all they needed to know. The receiver read the message, then returned the unopened letter to the letter carrier. So, the Post Office had carried the letter for nothing.

To solve this problem, Rowland Hill, a teacher who was interested in the mail service, suggested that the Post Office should carry *all* letters at the rate of one penny each, however far they went. The letters, said Hill, should be prepaid. This meant postage was paid by the sender, not the receiver of the letter.

The British government held a competition for the design of the new prepaid adhesive, or stick-on, stamps, but most of the designs sent in were far too complicated. Rowland Hill had a simple answer: The new stamps would carry just a portrait of the queen, Victoria. The result was the famous Penny Black, the world's first stamp, issued on May 6th, 1840.

It was a brillliant idea. One by one, other countries all over the world copied the simple new invention.

▷ This very early French envelope carries the 15-cent green stamp which was one value in the first seven issues of France in 1849. It shows the head of Ceres, the Roman goddess of the Earth. Later, Ceres appeared on many more definitive stamps of France.

▽ Charles Whiting entered this "essay" (**1**), or trial design, in the 1839 competition for the new British stamps. It was unsuccessful. Like other competitors, Whiting used the same kind of complicated design used on bank notes, which was meant to prevent forgeries.

△ Rowland Hill's design for the Penny Black (**2**) was also meant to prevent forgeries, even though it was much simpler than Charles Whiting's essay. Hill thought that people would notice any small differences between Queen Victoria's face on a forged stamp and on a real one.

▷ This is one of the U.S.A.'s first two stamps, issued in 1847. It shows George Washington, our first president. Benjamin Franklin, the first U.S. Postmaster-General, appeared on the other stamp, the five-cent brown. Washington and Franklin appeared in every U.S. definitive set until 1975.

2

▷ Bavaria was the first state to issue postage stamps in what is now Germany. This was the one-kreuzer black, issued in November 1849 (**1**). Although it issued its own stamps until 1920, Bavaria joined with other states to form a united Germany in 1870. The new country brought out its first stamp two years later, in 1872. One of these was the two-groschen blue (**2**).

1

△ Australia was much later with its first stamps than many other countries because the states that make up modern Australia did not join together until 1911. Australia's first stamp appeared in 1913, when a set of 15 values was printed. The stamp shown here is the highest value in the set, the £2 black and red. Collectors call this the "'roo" design. Can you see why? Australia was still issuing "'roo" stamps more than thirty years later in 1946.

◁ The first Dutch stamp, issued in 1852, was this five-cent blue, shown here in a block of four. The stamp carries a picture of the Dutch king, William III. Blocks of four became very popular after King George V of England started collecting stamps in this way.

2

1

▷ Naples, in southern Italy, was still a separate kingdom in 1858 when its first stamp, ½ torneso blue, was issued (**1**). Two years later, Naples and other Italian states were united into one country, Italy. In 1862 the Kingdom of Italy issued its first stamp, a 10-centisimi brown. This 1962 Italian "stamp-on-stamp" thematic (**2**) shows a picture of the first stamp at the top.

▽ The first Finnish stamp design of 1856 had a value in Russian kopeks. This was because Finland was a dukedom of Russia until 1917.

▷ A "stamp-on-stamp" thematic, like this Spanish one, is two stamps in one. This one shows the very first Spanish stamp, the 1850 six-cuartos black. It was issued in 1950 to commemorate one hundred years of Spanish stamps.

THE FIRST COLLECTORS

One day in 1841 a letter was published in a British newspaper, *The Times*, asking readers to send postage stamps to a young girl who was collecting them. That girl was probably the first collector of the new prepaid postage stamps, which had been issued the year before. In 1841 there were only three stamps to collect: the Penny Black, Twopenny Blue and Penny Red of Great Britain. So, the first collections held lots and lots of these few stamps.

But at first stamps were not put into albums—the first stamp album was not printed until 1862. Instead, stamps were often stuck on tables, chairs, walls or any other things in the home. One collector made a map of England and Wales using 2,139 stamps. Another covered a large screen with Indian and French stamps. Someone even made a wreath of leaves carrying the message "composed entirely of small portions of Napoleon III French stamps." A London dealer covered his office walls with 70,000 stamps. One of the most astonishing collections belonged to a circus performer named Albert Schafer, who decorated a whole room and its contents with thousands of stamps.

But rather than glue them to walls or trays, collectors soon began to take more care of their stamps. As more and more countries started issuing stamps, more and more people started collecting them. People soon realized that there were rare and common stamps. Some collectors found they could make a living buying and selling stamps. The first guide to prices, a stamp catalog, was published in 1863. Philately as we know it today was beginning to take shape.

▷ Albert Schafer put his own stamp portrait in his stamp room (**1**). He worked on the room while he recovered from falling off the high wire at the circus. Schafer used stamps to make the popular Chinese willow pattern on this plate (**2**). There were many other things decorated with stamps, including a whole tea service, as well as a guitar, a piano and this fireplace, mantlepiece and ship (**3**). The fireplace alone used up 3,000 stamps.

△ Jean-Baptiste Moens (1833-1908) was a very important man in philately —he was the first stamp dealer. He is shown here on a 1973 Belgian stamp commemorating the 50th anniversary of the Belgian Stamp Dealers' Association. He began selling stamps in 1852, from his book shop in Brussels, the Belgian capital. Later, Moens published catalogs and books about stamps and became a great expert on philately.

1

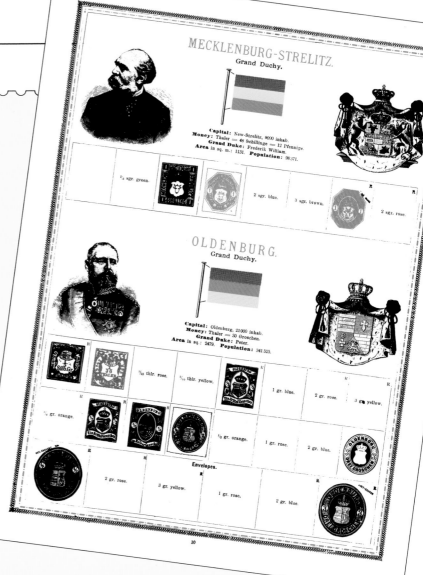

▷ A page from an 1892 stamp album. Mecklenburg-Strelitz and Oldenburg are now parts of Germany, but the album can, of course, still be used for the stamps issued by these two dukedoms. This album gave a great deal of useful information about countries. It did part of the work catalogs do today by printing pictures of stamps and showing how many stamps were in a set. It also told collectors if stamps were rare or common.

3

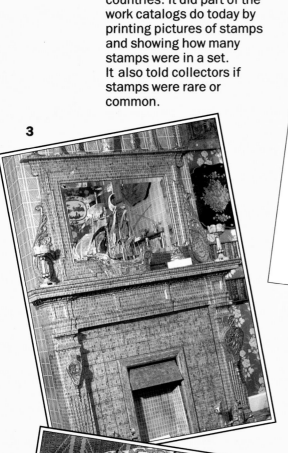

2

▽ This 19th-century luxury red leather stamp album is a work of art. The cover is beautifully inlaid with gold leaf decorations. Albums like this are collectors' items, especially in fine condition. Most collectors would have used plainer albums, like the one above.

WHAT SHALL I COLLECT?

All the world or one country?

Many people collect their own country's stamps. This is the easiest way to start. Stamp shops, stamp fairs and, of course, post offices have more of your own country's issues than any other country's.

But some collectors are more interested in foreign stamps because they may once have lived in that country or have relatives or friends there who send them stamps. You may prefer the designs or subjects seen on a foreign country's stamps or you may get interested in special sorts of stamps that some countries issue, such as Belgium's railway stamps or the U.S.A.'s airmails.

Some people try to collect the whole world. This is much harder than it used to be because since about 1950 more and more countries have been issuing more and more stamps. For example, in 1949 the U.S.A. issued 11 stamps. But in 1987 the U.S.A. issued 89 stamps! Even so, world collecting is a great challenge that offers fun and variety.

Fortunately, you can easily find out what suits you best. A good place to start is a catalog, particularly one illustrated in color, where you can see what a country's stamps look like. Magazines and books will also tell you a lot. Stamp clubs, exhibitions and other collectors will give you ideas. As long as you don't take up *too* much of their time, good dealers are usually very pleased to help and share their knowledge with you.

▷ People often collect commemoratives because they find them more attractive and interesting than definitives. This page from a collection of British commemoratives (**1**) includes two 1983 sets: a funfair issue and the Christmas set for that year, and the first 1984 set, which shows some coats of arms.

▷ Airmail issues often show aviation subjects, as you can see from this album page of U.S. airmail stamps from 1979 and 1980 (**3**). Airmails also show other subjects, though, such as the Statue of Liberty and the monument to four U.S. presidents at Mount Rushmore.

▷ Some collectors try to include all the stamps issued by a country. This page of French stamps (**2**) shows a mixture of definitives and commemoratives. The "Marianne" definitives are the six small stamps. The set of three large stamps on the line below comes from the beautiful French Art series which began in 1961.

◁ German stamps are fascinating because they show how much the country has changed since 1870: an 1865 stamp of Brunswick (**1**), a state that became part of a united Germany in 1870; a German Empire (1870–1918) stamp (**2**); a German Republic (1920–33) stamp (**3**); a Nazi (1933–45) stamp (**4**); a 1945 stamp issued by France (**5**), one of four countries that occupied Germany after 1945. Also shown here are recent stamps from West Germany (**6**), West Berlin (**7**) and East Germany (**8**).

WHAT SHALL I COLLECT?

Thematics

▽ The six stamps showing Disney characters, such as Mickey Mouse, are from different countries. There are hundreds of Disney "thematics," usually from small countries like the Maldive Islands in the Indian Ocean. The Dutch stamp (**1**) shows a cartoon from the "King and the Money Chest."

◁ Interested in space? You can collect hundreds of space stamps! Here are three—the Cuban one (**2**) shows Uri Gagarin, first man in space. The West German stamp (**3**) shows the space shuttle. The Hungarian stamp (**4**) illustrates "Flight to the Moon," by the French writer Jules Verne.

▽ The Boy Scouts is a worldwide organization, and scout stamps are issued by most countries. These two are from the Caribbean islands of Antigua (**8**) and Dominica (**9**). They show scouts hiking and practicing first aid. The Dominican scout gives the scout salute.

△ You'll never be short of stamps to collect if nature interests you. The Canadian stamp (**5**) is one of hundreds of beautiful flower stamps. How many dinosaurs can you recognize in the American stamp (**6**)? The unusual round stamp (**7**) shows New Zealand's national bird, the Kiwi.

Stamps are very versatile. They can show almost any subject that appeals to you. Are you interested in ships, aircraft, trains, birds, butterflies or pop stars? Hundreds of stamps picture these subjects and many, many more.

This kind of collecting—by subject or theme—is known as thematic or topical collecting. The first thematic is thought to be an 1860 train stamp from New Brunswick, Canada, though most thematics are more recent. In the 1920s and 1930s, stamps began to be printed by the "photogravure" process: This meant that a stamp design was photographed rather than engraved (cut) onto a steel or copper printing plate. It made it possible to print much more realistic pictures in many colors.

Photogravure allowed countries to present themselves on stamps better than ever before. A stamp could now "show off" its country's wildlife, scenery, costumes, works of art or national heroes. Collectors could see what a country was like without ever visiting it! For example, bullfighting is popular in Spain, so bulls and bullfighters often appear on Spanish stamps. Air transportation is vital in South America, where it is often the only way to reach one's destination. So, many South American stamps show aircraft, pilots or airfields, especially stamps from mountainous Chile or those from Brazil, which has vast areas of dense jungle.

1

2

3

4

△ The two French stamps shown here are transportation stamps and also postal history thematics. They show the mail being carried by ship (**1**) and bicycle (**2**). The German stamp (**3**) commemorates the 150th anniversary of German railways. Concorde, shown on a British stamp of 1969 (**4**), is the birdlike aircraft that can fly faster than the speed of sound. The Monaco stamp comes from a set of fourteen featuring old veteran cars (**5**) built between 1894 and 1910.

5

△ In 1971 Mali issued this stamp showing the French passenger liner "Normandie." It was one in a set of ships. "Normandie" was especially famous among the ships carrying passengers across the Atlantic Ocean. In 1935 the liner won the Blue Riband, a prize for the fastest Atlantic crossing, on her maiden (first) voyage.

◁ This 1975 stamp from Papua New Guinea, in the southwestern Pacific Ocean, shows a racing canoe. You can almost feel the speed of it as it cuts through the water. The fierce-looking figurehead at the prow, or front, of the canoe is meant to frighten the spirits, or gods, of the sea so that they will not harm the canoe.

▽ This submarine appears on a stamp in a 1982 set of Soviet naval ships, issued by Russia. Other stamps in the set show a mine-layer, a mine-sweeper, a cruiser and a battleship.

▽ The hydrofoil gunboat on this 1977 Italian stamp travels very fast by raising itself up on "legs" and skimming across the water surface. The stamp is one of a series of sets issued between 1977 and 1980 that show shipbuilding in Italy.

△ This is the highest value of four stamps in a British set issued to celebrate sailing. The stamp shows "multi-hulls," or yachts with more than one hull.

△ This stamp marks the 25th anniversary of the Pacific island of Hawaii becoming the 50th U.S. state. It shows a long distance, ocean-sailing canoe.

△ The Tall Ships race is held for old sailing ships like the one on this Finnish stamp issued for the 1972 race. This ship had many more sails than ordinary ships, which meant it could catch more wind and travel faster. It was a clipper ship, named because its speed allowed it to set new records by clipping time off the fastest journeys that had been made before.

▽ Norway is very mountainous. Most of its big towns are on the coast. Before there were good roads, it was easiest to go from town to town by ship. This Norwegian stamp shows an old coastal ship. It kept close to the coast and you can tell this from the birds on the stamp— they were usually a sure sign land was near.

WHAT SHALL I COLLECT?

Themes in themes

Collecting thematics can be much more than just finding as many stamps as possible on your theme. You can make collections within collections, breaking down big areas into smaller, more specialized themes. As you can see from the stamps shown on these pages, you could start collecting general transportation stamps. But there are thousands of stamps showing different types of transportation, and you might like to narrow your collection down to water transportation. You could go further and collect only stamps showing boats with sails. You could even specialize in, say, sailing boats used for pleasure.

You can do this with other themes. Animal stamps, for example, could be sorted into land animals, fish and other water creatures, insects and birds. From all these you might choose land animals, which could include animals found only in Australia and New Zealand, such as kangaroos, koala bears and the strange platypuses. Another way to divide the animal kingdom is to use the same method as scientists use and collect mammals, birds, fish, amphibia (animals like frogs and newts), reptiles or invertebrates (animals without backbones, such as insects). Possibly the most popular animal thematic speciality is prehistoric creatures, where there are plenty of stamps to choose from.

In the same way, you could collect flowers and specialize in roses or orchids. Or you could start with a general music theme and go on to concentrate on opera or the work of your favorite composer. Like so much in stamp collecting, the possibilities are almost endless.

◁ This 1975 stamp shows a traditional Japanese sailing ship. Ships like this were mainly used by fishermen. They were built so that they could not sail far from the Japanese coast. This was because, in 1636, an Isolation Decree, or law, prevented the Japanese from visiting other countries. The government feared its people might learn bad habits from foreigners.

STORIES IN STAMPS

△ These two U.S. stamps show Pony Express messengers carrying letters. Sending a letter by a messenger on horseback was the only speedy way to send mail where there were no railroads. When his horse got tired, the rider exchanged it for a fresh one.

You can learn about almost anything from stamps. They can tell the story of space travel, from Jules Verne's science fiction to modern rockets or satellites, or reveal a great deal about the Earth, with stamps showing minerals, volcanoes, oceans and even the Earth as it was millions of years ago.

When you've chosen a subject, you'll need to find out all you can about it—a local library is best for this. Before you search the catalogs, make a list of what you want to show. Some catalogs have lists of subjects shown on stamps, which makes the hunt easier. If, for example, your subject is the discovery of the Americas by Europeans, you'll need to know the explorers' names and when and where they lived. Spanish explorers were very important, so Spain has issued many stamps about the people and places involved. Many other countries took part too. For example, in 1534 Jacques Cartier, a Frenchman, sailed up the St. Lawrence, in what we now call Canada, and in 1984 a French stamp celebrated the 450th anniversary of his journey. Stamps aren't always issued on anniversaries, but dates of events or people's births or deaths may help you find stamps. Naturally, South and North American countries have themselves issued many stamps about exploration.

If you don't have a subject of your own, omnibus stamps (pages 72 and 73) can start you off with ideas and lots of stamps.

▽ This letter was mailed in 1861 in San Francisco, on the west coast of the U.S., and sent to Washington D.C., about 4,000 kilometers to the east. Part of its journey was by Pony Express. As well as an ordinary ten-cent U.S. stamp, you can see the special red one-dollar Pony Express stamp issued by Wells Fargo, the company that ran the service. One dollar was a lot of money in those days and when a railroad connected the east and west coasts it meant mail could be sent more cheaply and quickly by rail. The messenger services could not compete and eventually they were all put out of business by the railroads.

▽ This stamp shows the ceremony that marked the completion of the first railroad to join the east and west coasts of America. The ceremony was held on May 10, 1869, at Promontory Point, Utah. A special golden spike was used to nail the last piece of rail to a wooden tie.

My Vacation around Spain

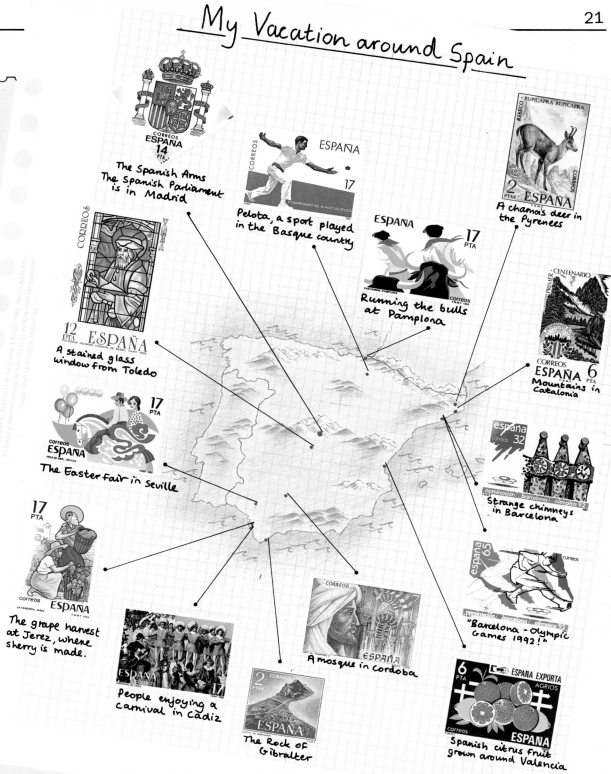

The Spanish Arms
The Spanish Parliament
is in Madrid

Pelota, a sport played
in the Basque country

A chamois deer in
the Pyrenees

A stained glass
window from Toledo

Running the bulls
at Pamplona

Mountains in
Catalonia

The Easter Fair in Seville

Strange chimneys
in Barcelona

The grape harvest
at Jerez, where
sherry is made.

People enjoying a
carnival in Cadiz

A mosque in Cordoba

"Barcelona - Olympic
Games 1992!"

The Rock of
Gibralter

Spanish citrus fruit
grown around Valencia

△ If you go on vacation in a foreign country, why
not make a stamp souvenir? You could draw a
simple map of the country on an album page
and mount the stamps around it, using arrows
to indicate the parts of the country they show.
Get a good mix of subjects, costumes, sports,
animals, buildings, flags, food, and so on.

△ This block of mint 1881 Penny Reds is overprinted "Cyprus" because the stamps were not meant for use in Britain but in Cyprus, an island in the Mediterranean that was then a British colony. We have enlarged part of a stamp to show its plate number. These stamps were made from different printing plates and each one was numbered. The plate numbers ran from 71 to 225. Some numbers are worth a fortune, others a few cents. A magnifying glass will tell you if you have a fortune in your tweezers!

▽ Another way to collect stamps is "on cover," or still on envelopes or cards. This letter was mailed in America with U.S. stamps. It crossed the Atlantic on board a ship carrying mail and arrived at Liverpool, England. It must have had too few U.S. stamps on it, for extra British Penny Reds were added before it was delivered to Fifeshire, Scotland.

MINT OR USED?

◁ Large, heavy postmarks were normal in the last century, so a "very fine used" stamp like this one was unusual. The cancel that made this postmark was possibly under-inked.

◁ This "fine used" Penny Red is also unusual, even though the postmark is heavily inked. As on the very fine used stamp, though, you can still see Queen Victoria's face clearly.

◁ The postmark on this "average used" stamp is very heavy and covers more of Victoria's face. This postmark is "average" because most Penny Reds were canceled like this.

◁ This stamp is "good used," which is rather a surprise since the face is almost hidden by a "Town" postmark, whose clear bars and town number would interest postmark collectors.

◁ This stamp is "poor used." It would be hard to find a heavier postmark than this. The face is totally hidden by a very thick, black "lozenge" postmark.

Which kinds of stamps should you collect, mint or used? Mint stamps—unused stamps which still have gum on the back—often cost more than used ones. Used stamps are not as clean as mint ones but they may have interesting or attractive postmarks that can tell you a lot more about how the stamp was used. But if you can afford it, the important thing is to collect what's attractive to you.

A mint stamp is usually nice and clean and you can see the picture clearly. Colors on a mint stamp are often brighter because, unlike used ones, they haven't gotten grubby in the mail nor have they been soaked in water to get them off envelopes. If a mint stamp is mounted, though, the hinge can make a nasty mark on the back. Sometimes the gum on the back of an old stamp goes yellow with age, and this may show through on the front. Always protect the gum on a mint stamp—the more damage to the gum, the lower the value of an unused stamp.

Collectors often like used stamps because a postmark shows the stamp has done the job it was supposed to do —paid for the postage on a letter or, as collectors say, it has "been somewhere." Not all used stamps are attractive. In fact, there are many different conditions in which you can find a used stamp, ranging from one with a very light postmark to one that's so heavily postmarked you can hardly see the picture on the stamp.

You can see, then, that there are good and bad mint and used stamps. So, before you buy them, look at them carefully to make sure they are good enough for your collection. This chapter is illustrated with just Great Britain's Penny Red so that you can compare heavily used and mint versions of the same stamp.

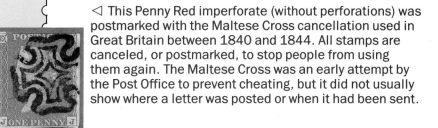

◁ This Penny Red imperforate (without perforations) was postmarked with the Maltese Cross cancellation used in Great Britain between 1840 and 1844. All stamps are canceled, or postmarked, to stop people from using them again. The Maltese Cross was an early attempt by the Post Office to prevent cheating, but it did not usually show where a letter was posted or when it had been sent.

WHAT STAMPS TELL YOU

Stamps on letters can travel all over the world and be seen by millions of people. This makes them an excellent way to inexpensively "advertise" a country. Italy, for example, makes cars, and to encourage people to buy more Italian cars, they often appear on Italy's stamps. Spain grows lots of fruit, vegetables and nuts, so you'll find Spanish stamps that show the country's crops. Countries often use their stamps to show off the great paintings of their artists or the discoveries of their scientists and explorers.

France, Mexico and Italy are among the many countries that issue special tourist stamps to publicize buildings, towns or beautiful scenery that attract visitors. Sometimes a country holds a big exhibition or meeting or is chosen to hold a big sports event. It usually issues stamps to remind everybody that, for example, soccer's World Cup was held in Italy in 1990.

All countries are made of small regions, and people in one area may have very different customs from people in another. In Spain, for example, people in one region don't always speak the same language as people in another. Spain has issued many stamps of traditional costumes from all over the country, and these could make an attractive collection to show some of the differences between the regions.

Stamps can tell you so much about a foreign country that you could almost take a vacation there without ever having to leave your stamp album!

△ St. Lucia is a volcanic island in the Caribbean. The two small mountains shown on this 1970 stamp are named the Pitons. They rise straight up out of the sea on the coast of St. Lucia. The Pitons are the special feature of the island and are seen on other St. Lucia stamps.

▽ The Netherlands probably has more windmills than anywhere else in the world. Most of the country is below sea level and there is always the danger of flooding. Wind can easily blow across the flat country and it is used to propel windmills, which drive water pumps that stop the land from flooding. This stamp shows a common type of windmill found in the Netherlands.

▷ Every February, Rio de Janeiro, in Brazil, holds its Carioca Carnival, when the city streets are filled with giant carnival floats, bands of musicians and dancing people dressed in fantastic costumes. The clowns shown on this Brazilian stamp of 1970 show how colorful these costumes can be.

▷ France is famous for its food and wonderfully tasty cooking. This 1980 stamp issued for a Gastronomical Exhibition (**1**), an exhibition for people interested in good food, shows a delicious French meal laid out as you might see it in a restaurant. It includes *l'angouste* (lobster), *gateaux* (cakes) and a *carafe* (glass jug) of wine.

In 1986 France issued a stamp to celebrate the Venetian Carnival in Paris (**2**), one of a regular series of foreign festivals that take place in the French capital. Venice is in northern Italy, but you can tell this is Paris because the Eiffel Tower, a famous Parisian landmark, can be seen behind the masked dancers.

1

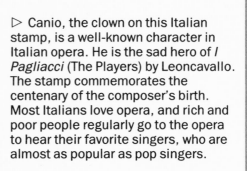

2

▷ Canio, the clown on this Italian stamp, is a well-known character in Italian opera. He is the sad hero of *I Pagliacci* (The Players) by Leoncavallo. The stamp commemorates the centenary of the composer's birth. Most Italians love opera, and rich and poor people regularly go to the opera to hear their favorite singers, who are almost as popular as pop singers.

▽ What do jazz music and the Statue of Liberty have in common? Both are special to the United States. Jazz began in the U.S., probably in the early 1900s. Jazz musicians like Duke Ellington, shown on a 1986 U.S. stamp, became famous all over the world. The Statue of Liberty, shown on a 1972 U.S. stamp, was a gift from France in 1886.

▷ Part of northern Scandinavia lies inside the Arctic Circle, where it is very cold and snowy. Many people live there, though, and in 1970, the Swedes issued a strip of stamps showing "Sweden within the Arctic Circle." These stamps show some Arctic wildlife, a herd of reindeer. They also show an easy way to travel in these frozen regions—on skis.

STRANGE STAMP STORIES

▷ The killing of Gaston Leroux was fortunately the only murder committed for the sake of a stamp. (You can see one of these stamps on page 57.) Later, after being found guilty at his trial, Giroux was executed for his crime.

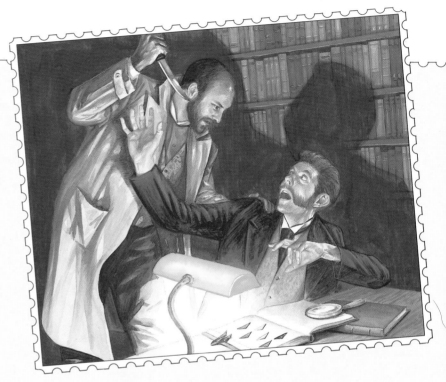

▽ Many of the envelopes found in an Ann Arbor street had one of the world's rarest stamps on them. Unfortunately people who do not know about stamps often throw them away. Often, the mistake is never discovered.

△ In 1900 Nicaragua issued two stamps showing the volcano Mount Momotombo erupting. The volcano was dormant, which meant it had not erupted for a long time. Even so, the picture on the stamp worried engineers planning to cut a canal nearby to join the Atlantic and Pacific oceans. Instead, the canal was cut further south, in Panama. The stamp was not the only reason for this change of plan, but it helped!
The picture is from a card in a series that was given away in cigarette packets. It shows one of the stamps and a ship in the Panama Canal.

There are many strange stamp stories and many of them are about lucky or unusual finds. For example, in 1874 some very valuable stamps—three pfennig reds of Saxony—were found stuck to a ceiling beam in a farmer's house in Eibenstock, Germany. The farmer's father had been a postmaster and stuck the stamps there as souvenirs!

In 1939, in Ann Arbor, Michigan, valuable covers (envelopes) were found blowing around on the street. Some workers had dumped piles of old papers outside a house they were clearing out. A wind blew up and scattered the papers. Fortunately, they were seen by a knowledgeable collector. He took one look at the covers, then rushed over to the trashbin and rescued as many as he could. Why did the collector get so excited? Because some of the covers carried the famous New York Provisional Postmasters' stamps, issued before the first official U.S. stamps of 1847.

Not all strange stamp stories have happy endings, though. One stamp, in fact, led to a murder.

The killing happened in Paris, France, in 1892. A rich collector named Gaston Leroux had in his collection the world's one and only unused 1851 two-cent "Missionary" issue of Hawaii. One day Leroux was found stabbed to death in his apartment. The police could not at first discover why he had been killed. Then they found that the Hawaiian stamp was missing from his album. When the police investigated the people who had known Leroux, they began to suspect a friend of his, another collector named Hector Giroux. But they had no proof that Giroux was guilty.

So a detective pretended to be a collector, and became friendly with Giroux. After a time, he tricked Giroux into boasting about the mint Missionary stamp in his collection. Since only one of these stamps was known to exist, it must have been Leroux's and there was only one way Giroux could have come by it. Giroux was arrested and confessed to the murder. He had tried to persuade Leroux to sell him the stamp. When Leroux refused, Giroux killed him.

◁ A Leipzig dealer discovered rare stamps in a farmhouse. He carefully removed the stamps, which were later sold to Philippe von Ferrary.

THE BRITISH ROYAL COLLECTION

Britain's King George VI (**1**) was a keen collector and found much comfort in the Royal Collection in the difficult years of World War II. The collection of British and Commonwealth stamps is one of the world's greatest and is kept in more than 325 albums and many bookcases in a room in Buckingham Palace in London. It was begun by George VI's father, George V, after his uncles gave him some stamps.

One of Britain's rarest stamps is the only used copy of the King Edward VII two-penny Tyrian Plum, shown here with mint copies on a page from the Royal Collection (**2**). King Edward died the day it was to be issued, May 6, 1910. The day before, someone in the Post Office sent it on a letter to the king's son, Prince George, knowing he would be delighted to own the first used copy of the stamp. The prince got the letter the next day. But before the day was over, he was the new king, George V, for his father, King Edward, had died just before midnight.

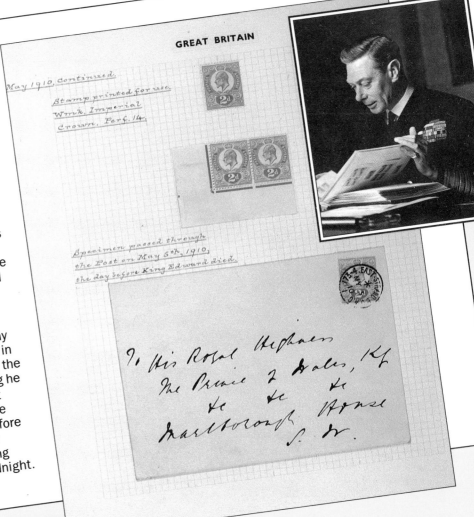

GREAT BRITAIN

May 1910, continued.

Stamp printed for use.

Wmk. Imperial Crown. Perf. 14.

Specimen passed through the Post on May 6th, 1910, the day before King Edward died.

To His Royal Highness
The Prince of Wales, Kg
&c &c &c
Marlborough House
S. W.

◁ This is how some royal collectors appeared on stamps of their own countries: King Carol of Romania (**1**); King Hussein of Jordan (**2**); King George V of England (**3**) and his son, King George VI (**4**); Prince Rainier of Monaco (**5**). The Spanish King Alfonso XIII (**6**) is shown on the right of the stamp, at the first Spanish National Philatelic Stamp Exhibition in 1930. King Farouk of Egypt (**7**) is shown next to his father, King Faud (**8**). Not a king, but probably richer than some kings, the famous collector Philippe von Ferrary (**9**) is shown (neatly dressed!) on a Leichtenstein stamp.

FAMOUS COLLECTORS

△ Philippe von Ferrary, dressed as a tramp, bids for an expensive stamp at an auction.

▽ U.S. President Roosevelt is shown with his collection on this stamp of Monaco, issued for a philatelic exhibition held to mark the centenary of U.S. stamps. Like King George VI, Roosevelt found great comfort in his stamps during the dangerous wartime years when he was president. Several other countries have issued stamps showing Roosevelt as a collector. He was such an enthusiast that he even designed some U.S. stamps, the 1934 Special Delivery airmail stamps.

In the early 1900s a shabby man in an old torn suit and a greasy beret was often seen at stamp auctions. He looked like a tramp, but when other collectors saw him they knew they had no hope of competing with him for the rare stamps on sale. The "tramp" was actually one of the world's richest men, Philippe von Ferrary. Ferrary spent most of his huge fortune on stamps and traveled all over Europe to stamp auctions. He may have dressed strangely, but he had a wonderful collection, which included the world's most valuable stamp, the 1856 British Guiana one-cent magenta.

Many rich people have been keen stamp collectors and, like Ferrary, they did some strange things for the sake of their collections. In 1922, the American millionaire Alfred Hind bought Ferrary's British Guiana stamp at an auction. It was thought to be the only copy in the world. Later, Hind discovered *another* copy in Paris. He bought it for a huge sum of money and then he burned it so that his first copy would still be the only one in the world.

Another American, Colonel Green, also spent fortunes on stamps. Once, Green thought he had been cheated over a stamp. So, to check the stamp more closely, he ordered a huge magnifying glass which could enlarge stamps over two thousand times. It was a meter thick and so big that a door had to be removed before it could be taken into Green's house.

STAMP ALPHABETS AND OTHER MYSTERIES

The Latin, or Roman, alphabet, in which this book is printed, is the world's most widely used alphabet. Most stamps use the Latin, and are usually easy to read. Even so, you will find many stamps that have no Latin lettering on them, and where they come from may be a mystery. For example, Russian, Bulgarian and some Yugoslav stamps use the Cyrillic alphabet. Russian stamps say "CCCP," which in Cyrillic reads "SSSR," meaning the Union of Soviet Socialist Republics.

Greek stamps use the Greek alphabet, but fortunately, recent issues also say "Hellas," the Greek name for Greece. Other countries that use non-Latin alphabets include Japan, China, Korea and three territories, once independent, that are now part of Yugoslavia—Montenegro, Serbia and Croatia.

Luckily, you don't have to read these alphabets or languages to recognize the country name of a stamp. If you look at stamp catalogs, you'll see pictures of these stamps there. Copy out the country name in their own lettering, with your "translation" of the name beside it. Look at your list whenever you come across a stamp inscribed in a strange alphabet.

Because Latin alphabet countries like Austria, Switzerland, Spain, Hungary and many more have their own names for their countries, or just use initials, it's a good idea to copy these out, too.

△ Greek stamps did not show "Hellas" (Greece) in Latin letters until 1966, over 100 years after the first Greek stamp. So about 1,000 Greek stamps are marked with "Hellas" in Greek letters only (along the top). This is a 1939 stamp.

▽ Look carefully to identify stamps of Communist China. Find the first Chinese character, a rectangle with a line through it. On the smaller stamp we have enlarged it for you. Look for it on the long stamp showing an ancient Chinese procession.

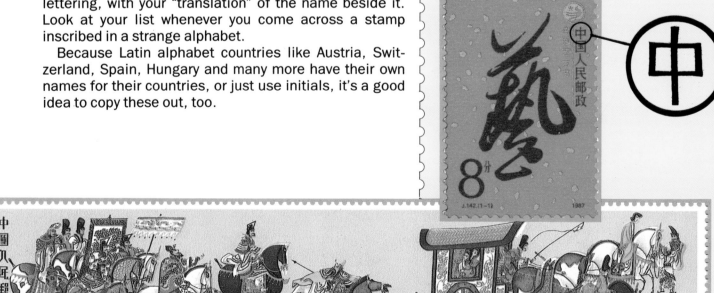

▷ Some countries are identified by initials. This miniature sheet of stamps is from East Germany (DDR, or Deutsche Demokratische Republik). Another is KSA (Kingdom of Saudi Arabia).

△ After the 1917 Russian Revolution, Ukraine declared independence and issued its own stamps, marked only in Cyrillic letters; but you can spot a Ukranian stamp by a trident symbol, left of the face. In 1923 Ukraine became part of the U.S.S.R. and it stopped issuing stamps.

◁ The bottom words on this stamp say "Bulgarian Post" in Cyrillic lettering. The stamp's value is CT 20, or 20 stotinki in Bulgarian money.

△ This stamp shows its country's name twice. At the bottom it's printed in Latin letters— "Nippon" is Japanese for Japan. At the top it appears in Japanese characters. Japanese stamps have been marked like this since 1966.

◁ This stamp from Laos, in Southeast Asia, shows its country in Laotian at the top left and in Latin letters as "Postes Lao" (French for Laos Post—Laos was once ruled by France, so French is the second language there).

PHILATELICALLY TERMINATED

△ In 1861, 11 southern states split away from the United States to rule themselves. This led to the bloody Civil War between the Southern Confederate States and the Northern states, who wanted the states to stay together in a "Union." Jefferson Davis, shown on the Confederate stamp (**1**), was briefly president of the breakaway states. The Confederates lost the war in 1865 and their stamps were no longer issued. The envelope (**2**), with an 1861 U.S. stamp, shows the Union flag and a motto supporting the Union side.

▽ This 1981 strip of map stamps (**1**) shows how the various Canadian states joined together to form Canada. British Columbia/Vancouver Island joined the Union of Canada in 1871. You can see the territory marked on the first stamp in the strip. In 1962 Canada commemorated the founding of Victoria, capital of British Columbia a century before, with a stamp showing the state's first stamp (**2**) from 1860. Canada was not complete until 1949, when Newfoundland joined. Newfoundland's last stamp of its own (**3**), issued in 1947, commemorated its discoverer, Matthew Cabot.

△ These stamps show what happened when the British colony of the Gold Coast (**1**) became independent Ghana. The overprinted stamp of the Gold Coast (**2**) was used in Ghana for six months until the first Ghanaian stamp was issued. The Ghanaian stamp (**3**) was issued two years after independence.

When you look through a stamp catalog, you will find many countries that no longer exist. These are "philatelically terminated" countries. This sounds rather scary, but all it means is that these countries no longer issue stamps.

A country can be philatelically terminated for many different reasons. Some, like Ceylon, which became Sri Lanka in 1972, simply change their names. Others were once colonies ruled by another country, often thousands of miles away. Most of these countries are now independent and rule themselves. To show their independence they may change their name. The Gold Coast in western Africa, for instance, was once a colony in the British Empire. But since it became independent in 1957, it has been called Ghana instead.

Some places that once issued their own stamps have become part of other countries. Hawaii, for instance, once had its own stamps. Now Hawaii uses U.S. stamps. Tibet, in Asia, once independent with its own stamps, is now part of China.

A few countries, such as Germany, Italy, Canada and Australia, were once groups of small states. So, the first stamps from these parts of the world carry the names of these small states. Later, when the states joined together to form bigger countries, their stamps carried the new countries' names.

Sometimes large countries split up into two or more smaller countries. For example, in 1975 the Gilbert and Ellice Islands were divided into two separate countries, Tuvalu and Vanuatu, which became two new stamp-issuing countries, while the Gilbert and Ellice Islands became philatelically terminated.

◁ Tangier, a town in Morocco, North Africa, became an International Zone in 1923, and was ruled by three countries: Great Britain, France and Spain. Each country had post offices there and each printed special stamps for use in Tangier. Here are some of them—a Spanish telegraph stamp (**1**), an overprinted French postage due (**2**) and an overprinted British commemorative (**3**). Tangier was philatelically terminated when Morocco became independent in 1956 and issued the first Moroccan stamps.

◁ These U.S. stamps are definitive stamps with a difference. They are "non-denominational" stamps, which means they have no value printed on them, just a letter C. This shows they can be used only for letters mailed to places inside the U.S. This was done because the stamps' price might have gone up. Instead of printing new stamps with new values, the same stamps could still be used but sold at the higher price. Britain and France have also issued stamps like these.

△ This is a 1964 French military frank stamp. It has no value printed on it because a letter with this sort of stamp can go through the mail free of charge. The letters are written by soldiers and other servicemen living away from home. France has issued stamps for this purpose since 1901. This one shows the *Tricolor* ("three color"), the flag of France.

◁ In 1935 Astrid, the beautiful young Queen of Belgium, was killed in a car crash. Belgium issued a set of mourning stamps to commemorate this tragic event. Mourning stamps have black borders to show sadness.

△ Mercury, shown here on a 1918 Austrian newspaper stamp, was the messenger of the ancient Roman gods. As a speedy deliverer of news and information, Mercury was a good image to have on newspaper stamps. These were special stamps for sending magazines and newspapers through the mail. Austria printed Mercury on most newspaper stamps, which were issued between 1851 and 1921.

△ Italy issued this stamp in 1965 to commemorate its night airmail postal service.

△ This 1922 U.S. special delivery stamp shows a letter being delivered by motorcycle to get it to its destination as quickly as possible. Special delivery costs more than ordinary letter delivery.

▽ This Italian stamp, showing the head of King Victor Emmanuel III, was for express letter post to foreign countries.

△ This is a postage due stamp of the Wallis and Futuna Islands. It was issued in 1930, when the islands were part of a French colony in the Pacific Ocean. The stamp was originally issued for New Caledonia, another French Pacific colony, but the overprint turned it into a stamp from a different country, Wallis and Futuna.

WHY STAMPS ARE ISSUED

Stamps are issued for many different purposes. Some, called definitives, are ordinary stamps that are always in use for mailing letters or parcels. France, for instance, has issued millions of definitive stamps showing imaginary characters from myths and legends, including Ceres, Sabine, Marianne and Mercury. Great Britain's "Machin" definitives were first issued in 1967. They show the head of Queen Elizabeth II and are still in use more than twenty years later. (The stamps were based on Arnold Machin's design for a medal showing the queen's head.)

Commemorative stamps are issued for special events like anniversaries. Unlike definitives, they are usually sold in post offices for only a short time. Commemoratives are often larger than definitives and usually have a special picture on them.

Postage due stamps are put on letters that do not have enough ordinary stamps to pay the postage. The receiver of the letter pays the extra amount shown on the postage dues.

Some countries issue parcel post stamps, and there are also stamps that cost more than ordinary stamps but speed up the sorting and delivery of mail. Special delivery and express mail stamps are common examples of these. Some countries, like Austria or Brazil, have used special stamps for mailing newspapers cheaply. Belgium still uses railway stamps for mail carried by train. Finally, there are hundreds of different types of official or service stamps that were specially printed for use by government departments.

▽ These are Italian parcel post stamps; the sender of the parcel put the left-hand stamp on the parcel to pay the postage. The right-hand stamp was kept as a receipt, or a ticket to show that the post office had taken the parcel, in case it got lost. These stamps were first issued in 1914.

△ An artist at work painting a butterfly for a stamp.

△ Correcting tiny errors on a photogravure stamp printing cylinder.

▷ Drilling holes on a new perforating cylinder. The work has to be extremely accurate and a computer controls the drilling machine.

1

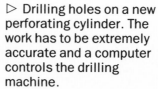

◁ Many stamps seem to show all the colors of the rainbow. In fact, most stamps are printed from just four colors: blue, red, yellow and black. Before printing a picture, a special machine makes four different photographs of it, one for each color. These are used to make printing plates for each color. Under a magnifying glass you'll see each photograph is made up of thousands of tiny blue, red, yellow and black dots. Printed one on top of the other, the dots mix together so you see the original picture's colors. This special set of stamps shows three of the colors that make up the final stamp. Yellow is not shown alone but is printed with the blue (**1**) and red (**2**). Look at the van in the last stamp and in the other stamps. What do you notice?

2

△ These rough sketches were done for a 1911 competition to design the first definitive stamps of South Africa. Sketches like these save time. Later, the artist will spend more time turning the sketches into neat designs.

△ This huge modern stamp printing press can print up to ten million stamps an hour and can print them in ten different colors.

◁ This German stamp shows stamps coming off a printing machine on a long roll of paper.

△ Checking the stamps before they are sent out to post offices.

HOW STAMPS ARE MADE 1

From paintbrush to post office

Many people's careful work and attention is needed to produce a stamp. First, a group of people decide what will be shown on the stamp. Next, several designers are asked to draw designs for the stamp, which may be illustrated with a photograph or a painting. When the best design is chosen and the illustration is ready, lettering is added to indicate things such as the stamp's value.

If the stamp is engraved, the illustration now goes to an engraver, who uses a tool to engrave the design, stamp size, onto a polished steel block. Other ways of printing stamps use special photographic machines to copy and reduce the stamp design to stamp size. Whichever printing method is used, the next stage is to print a "proof" on a small press. The proof looks like a stamp but has no perforations. It is compared with the original design to check that it has been properly copied and printed. If anything is wrong, it is sent back to the printer to be corrected.

Now we are nearly ready to print the stamps. A full sheet may contain over 200 stamps, so a special machine copies the stamps into neat rows, either onto a large piece of film ready to make a printing plate or directly on to the plate. The printing plate is usually in the form of a roller so that stamps can be printed nonstop on a long roll of paper, which is later cut into sheets. Modern machines can print millions of stamps an hour.

After the stamps are printed they pass between two rollers. One roller has neat rows of holes, the other has rows of needles that exactly match the holes in the other roller. As the rollers turn, the needles are forced through the stamp sheet and into the holes, leaving neatly perforated stamps.

Finally, the stamps are carefully checked for any errors. Stamp collectors are delighted to find errors, but the printer hates to let any escape!

◁ The larger picture shows an artist's painting of a baseball player. Beside it, you can see the final U.S. stamp, with lettering added.

HOW STAMPS ARE MADE 2

Different ways to print stamps

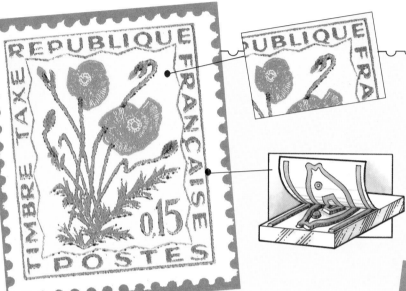

◁ This French postage due stamp was originally printed by letterpress. You can see that the printing is not as good as that of the other stamps on these pages. You can often spot letterpress stamps by looking at edges of the printed parts. If there is too much ink on a letterpress plate, the extra ink is squeezed to the edges of the raised printing parts. Under a magnifying glass, you can see this as uneven, darker patches of color.

▷ This stamp was originally litho-printed, like the whole of this book. "Litho" stamps can be brightly colored, but most of the colors come from tiny dots printed in just a few colors which, when seen together, appear to blend into many more colors. You can spot litho-printing by looking at the lettering under a magnifying glass; unlike gravure lettering, it will have even edges.

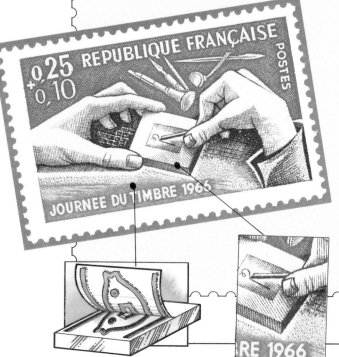

◁ The design of a recess-printed stamp is cut, or engraved, into a steel plate. These cuts are tiny grooves that fill up when the plate is covered with ink. A blade then wipes the plate clean, leaving ink only in the grooves. Paper is now forced against the plate. The ink sticks to the paper when it is pulled away, leaving tiny ink ridges you can often feel with your fingertips.

This French recess-printed stamp actually shows an engraver using a special tool to engrave a steel plate. Hand-engraving is more expensive than making a photogravure plate with a photographic machine.

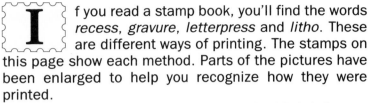

If you read a stamp book, you'll find the words *recess*, *gravure*, *letterpress* and *litho*. These are different ways of printing. The stamps on this page show each method. Parts of the pictures have been enlarged to help you recognize how they were printed.

A stamp is a piece of paper printed with ink from a printing plate. But ink does not cover the whole stamp—parts of it are just bare paper. So, a printing plate must have parts that print ink and parts that do not. Different ways of printing use different methods to keep ink on the printing parts but keep it off the non-printing parts of the plate.

The first stamps of 1840 were "recess-printed." Recess printing means that the printing part is sunk, or "recessed," below the surface of a plate. *"Intaglio,"* another word for recess printing, is still used by countries such as France and Austria for some stamps.

Gravure, short for "photogravure," is a modern version of recess printing. Instead of the lines that make up a recess design, a gravure picture is made up of millions of tiny dots that are printed from tiny "cells," or holes, sunk below the surface of the plate. These cells are the printing parts and are made by a photographic method.

Letterpress is the simplest way to print. The printing part is raised above the rest of the plate. "Surface printing," another term for letterpress, is rarely used today because the other methods print better-looking stamps.

Most modern stamps are printed by "offset lithography," "litho" for short. A litho plate is completely flat. Its printing part is treated with a special chemical that attracts ink. Ink will not stick to the other parts of the plate, so these do not print.

△ These Dutch stamps were originally printed by photogravure. Although gravure gives beautiful, rich colors that blend into each other very smoothly, the colors are actually made up from millions of tiny dots printed in just a few colors. These dots are printed by cells that cover the whole of the printing plate, including the lettering. So, if you want to see if a stamp is gravure-printed, look at the lettering under a magnifying glass. Instead of straight or curved edges, the letter edges are ragged where they have been broken up by the cells.

◁ Embossed stamps are made from two plates, but since no ink is used, it's not true printing. Imagine a mask that *exactly* fits around your face, with no gaps anywhere. One embossing plate has a design cut into it, like the mask's inside. The other plate has the same design, but raised up so it fits into the other plate, like your face into the mask. If a stamp is pressed between the plates, it is molded into the shape of the design. Embossing is slow and expensive and rarely used today.

◁ A few stamps are printed by two different processes. The ship on this stamp is recess-printed, but the face is gravure-printed.

STAMPS SEEN IN DIFFERENT WAYS

Some people never collect stamps and never stick them in albums. Instead, they collect stamps in different forms from the ordinary stamps we usually buy at post offices. Some collect British PHQ (Postal Headquarters) cards or "maximum" cards (maxicards) from countries like France, Germany or Japan. These are postcards illustrated with a stamp printed to the size of the card. The real stamp can be stuck to the enlarged stamp so that the whole card can be mailed and specially postmarked.

Miniature sheets and souvenir sheets have one or more stamps perforated into them, leaving wide borders for decoration or extra information about the stamps or the events they commemorate. Souvenir sheets are often given away free at stamp exhibitions. Not all of these stamps can be used to pay postage.

Presentation packs issued by the Post Office are sets of mint stamps mounted on a stock card in a special folder that tells you all about the stamps.

People also collect booklets of small sheets of stamps stitched into card covers. They may include mixtures of different value stamps and interesting advertisements or information about postal charges.

Many of these philatelic items are stiff and bulky. If you collect a large number of them, they are best protected in a special album with transparent covers. If you have just a few, however, you can use photographic corners (made for mounting photographs in photo albums) to mount them in ordinary stamp albums.

△ Look carefully to find the actual stamp in this miniature sheet from Sierra Leone — it's in the middle of the stained glass window. This sheet is one of four matching ones and shows how attractive stamps can look on a larger sheet. Plain miniature sheets are similar to this but the stamps are not perforated into the sheet.

△ This is an advertisement pane from a 1936 British stamp booklet that contained stamps of King Edward VIII. (A pane is a small sheet of stamps in a booklet or a part of a larger sheet.) "Cash's Satin Lingerie Ribbons" were cloth labels with your name woven into them. You sewed them into your clothes to show that they belonged to you.

▽ This souvenir sheet was printed to commemorate a German children's competition to design a stamp for the year 2000. The "stamp" could not be used to pay postage but it is still interesting to collectors. Souvenir sheets like this are usually issued for postal events such as exhibitions. Miniature sheets can also be used as souvenirs.

△ The set of stamps in this Swedish booklet shows old signs bakers or shoemakers, for example, used to hang outside their shops. Booklets are often sold from machines outside post offices and are a handy way to buy stamps. The stamp edges here are imperforate. This is not an error and happens when booklets are made.

▽ This is one of a set of PHQ cards issued in Great Britain in 1987 to commemorate the 300th anniversary of Isaac Newton's important book about physics. Newton is supposed to have discovered gravity when he saw an apple fall from a tree. Some PHQ or maxicards are used and franked with a postmark similar to the design of the stamp.

△ This strip of stamps was issued in 1987 by France for its overseas territory of St. Pierre and Miquelon, which lies off the coast of Canada. The three sections make a complete picture. Stamps arranged like this are called composites. The strip has been carefully designed so that when you take off the stamps at either end, each one makes a good picture on its own.

◁ This 1989 stamp from Israel has a perforated tab, or extra piece, at the bottom. Between 1893 and 1912 Belgium also issued stamps with tabs. Tabs are a useful way of extending a stamp to give it an extra decoration or to add some information about the subject of the stamp.

△ Some of the strangest stamps ever must be these "talking stamps" from Bhutan. Issued in 1973, they are printed on plastic and will actually play. The records play tunes like the national anthem (in English or in Bhutanese), local folk songs and even a talk about the history of Bhutan. There were seven stamps in the set and they were printed on red, blue, green, black or clear plastic.

△ Most stamps are printed on paper. However, in 1955 Hungary issued a stamp printed on aluminum foil to celebrate the Light Metal Industries Congress. Since then quite a few of these unusual stamps have been issued by countries such as Tonga, the U.S.S.R. and the Central African Republic, which issued this stamp, showing a space satellite, in 1982.

▽ Between 1969, when these banana-shaped stamps were issued, and 1985, Tonga issued more than 600 self-adhesive stamps. You simply peel off their backing paper and stick them on envelopes. Many of these stamps have unusual shapes—some are even shaped like watches or parrots!

STRANGE STAMPS

△ This Bhutan stamp of 1976 is printed on a special kind of plastic that gives the real stamp a 3-D appearance. Unfortunately, this book is printed on paper, so you can't see the true effect. This stamp is from a set of 11 stamps showing traditional ceremonial masks.

▽ If you find this 1956 Italian stamp, don't think you've found a rare error—it's meant to look like this! People were supposed to look at the stamp through a special set of glasses that would make the two parts of the design come together and give the stamp a 3-D appearance.

A glance through the pages of this book will tell you that most stamps are square or oblong in shape. However, there are many that are not, but are triangular, for example. The first triangle-shaped stamps were the 1853 issues of Cape of Good Hope. In 1930 Spain issued some triangular stamps that showed the three ships that took Columbus on his first voyage to America in 1492. These stamps were printed with a matching triangle of decorated paper, which actually turned them into diamond-shaped stamps. Other stamps have had oval or octagonal (eight-sided) shapes.

Stamps with peel-off protective paper over their sticky backs that need no licking have been issued in even stranger shapes. They include scrolls of paper, maps, fruit, and a 1970 Sierra Leone stamp in the shape of a jewel box containing a huge sparkling diamond.

Bhutan, a tiny kingdom high in the Himalayan mountains, has issued many unusual stamps. As well as stamps printed on plastic or foil, and 3-D stamps, a 1969 set was printed on silk cloth. Then there were some stamps showing roses. You might think there's nothing unusual about that, but these stamps actually smelled like roses!

Most of the stamps mentioned so far have been modern. However, in the 1920s, when there was a paper shortage, Latvia, now part of Russia, used up some sheets of banknotes that had been printed on one side only by printing stamps on the other side.

◁ Both these stamps have two sets of perforations, a normal set on the outside, and an unusually shaped one around the design. The stamp from Singapore (**1**) is perforated in a circle. The stamp from Gibraltar (**2**) is perforated in the shape of the famous Rock of Gibraltar that sticks out from the coast of southern Spain into the Mediterranean Sea.

COLLECTING COVERS

Cover is the collector's name for envelopes or postcards, and there are all sorts of interesting covers you can collect. "Commercial" covers are ordinary letters mailed every day in countries all over the world. An unusual combination of stamps on a commercial cover may make it worth keeping rather than soaking off the stamps.

Other covers are more special. First day covers, for example, carry new stamps posted on the first day of issue and often have special "first day" postmarks. They also usually have a specially printed cover. You can order first day covers from dealers or the Post Office. Special event covers are issued to celebrate the start of a new airline route or perhaps an expedition; they also have a special picture envelope but they use whatever stamps are available at the post office on that day.

A *paquebot* (packet boat) cover is the name of an envelope mailed on board a ship. In the same way, zeppelin covers were carried by zeppelin airships more than fifty years ago. People also collect postal stationery—postcards, unusual greetings cards, such as old Valentine cards, and envelopes or airletters with stamps already printed on them, ready for mailing.

Collecting covers is often called collecting postal history—that is, covers from the earlier days of postal services. Never remove a stamp from an old cover. It's much more interesting to keep it on the cover and it may make it more valuable! Very old covers can be much older than the first stamps and are called "pre-stamp" covers. Even though some pre-stamp covers are up to four hundred years old, they are not always expensive and can be found in good condition.

△ Soon after the first Penny Black was issued, this beautiful, hand-painted Valentine card was sent by a young man to his sweetheart, telling her how much he loved her.

▷ This registered letter was mailed in Sarawak, a small state protected by Britain, in Asia, which was then ruled by the so-called White Rajahs (a rajah was normally an Indian prince). Charles Brooke, the second rajah, appears on the Sarawak stamps. The letter also carries stamps from Straits Settlements, a nearby British colony. This was because the letter needed extra postage as it passed through on its way to Amsterdam.

1

2

△ This 1984 Swedish first day cover (**1**) celebrates the 100th anniversary of the Swedish Post Office Savings Bank. As well as a special postmark, the cover has a photograph of a savings book, where people kept a record of the money they had saved. The 1983 British first day cover (**2**) is for a set of stamps showing old and new army uniforms. It has a special postmark used only on the first day of issue.

△ The hovercraft travels very fast over land or water on a cushion of air. This 1968 "first flight" cover, with a French stamp, celebrates the start of the Channel Hovercraft Service between Dover, England, and Boulogne, France. This cover is similar to a first day cover but does not have a special stamp to mark the event.

1

2

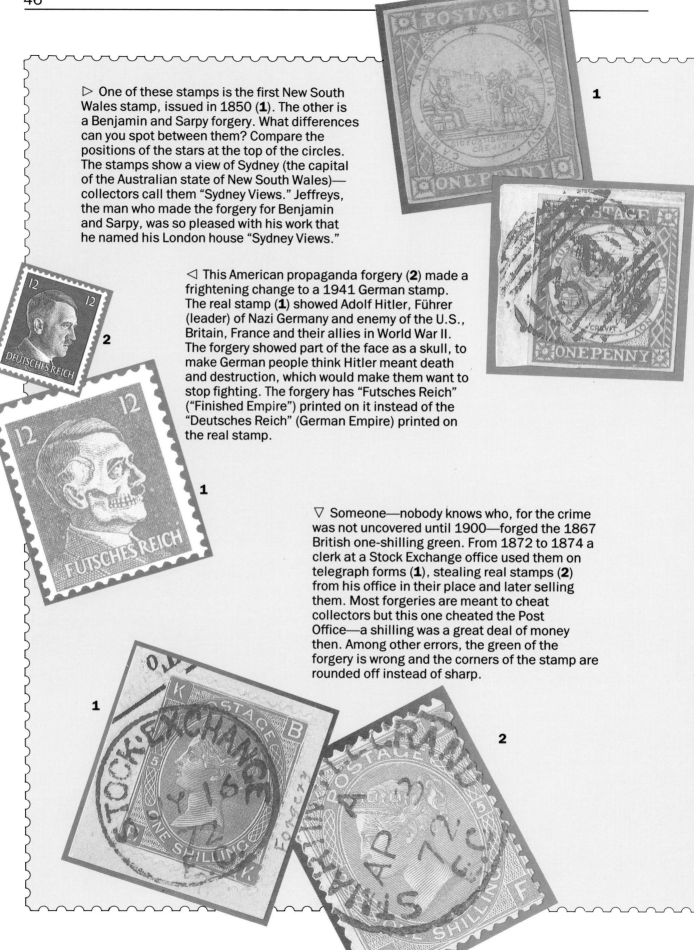

▷ One of these stamps is the first New South Wales stamp, issued in 1850 (**1**). The other is a Benjamin and Sarpy forgery. What differences can you spot between them? Compare the positions of the stars at the top of the circles. The stamps show a view of Sydney (the capital of the Australian state of New South Wales)—collectors call them "Sydney Views." Jeffreys, the man who made the forgery for Benjamin and Sarpy, was so pleased with his work that he named his London house "Sydney Views."

◁ This American propaganda forgery (**2**) made a frightening change to a 1941 German stamp. The real stamp (**1**) showed Adolf Hitler, Führer (leader) of Nazi Germany and enemy of the U.S., Britain, France and their allies in World War II. The forgery showed part of the face as a skull, to make German people think Hitler meant death and destruction, which would make them want to stop fighting. The forgery has "Futsches Reich" ("Finished Empire") printed on it instead of the "Deutsches Reich" (German Empire) printed on the real stamp.

▽ Someone—nobody knows who, for the crime was not uncovered until 1900—forged the 1867 British one-shilling green. From 1872 to 1874 a clerk at a Stock Exchange office used them on telegraph forms (**1**), stealing real stamps (**2**) from his office in their place and later selling them. Most forgeries are meant to cheat collectors but this one cheated the Post Office—a shilling was a great deal of money then. Among other errors, the green of the forgery is wrong and the corners of the stamp are rounded off instead of sharp.

FAMOUS FORGERS

Forgeries, or illegal copies of stamps, always worry collectors and Post Offices, and some forgers have become very famous. For example, a century ago in England, Benjamin and Sarpy ran a company to make "instant" copies of rarities. They took orders from collectors who could not afford the real stamps but preferred cheap copies to fill gaps on their album pages. Even so, Benjamin and Sarpy did cheat collectors and in 1891 they were sent to prison for forgery.

A Swiss forger, François Fournier, made dozens of copies of stamps every day in his workshop. He was so proud of his work that in 1910 he issued a catalog of his "stamps." The Philatelic Society of Geneva thought he was so dangerous that in 1928, after he died, they bought his equipment and destroyed it.

The cleverest forger of all was an Italian, Juan de Sperati, whose work was almost impossible to tell from the real thing. In 1942 he was arrested in France, accused of smuggling rare stamps out of the country. Experts said the stamps were real, but they were actually Sperati forgeries. To prove this, Sperati made some identical stamps while awaiting trial. He also claimed he had never sold his copies as real stamps, for he signed his name on their backs. So, he was found not guilty of either forgery or smuggling! But collectors are still wary of his work, for he signed his stamps with a soft pencil that was easily erased, leaving no sign to an unwary collector that the stamp was forged.

◁ The pair of stamps on the left are accurate, modern reproductions of an 1864 Mexican stamp, showing Maximilian, the Austrian Archduke who ruled Mexico at this time. Reproductions are not dishonest forgeries unless someone tries to sell them as real stamps. They are intended for collectors who cannot afford the real stamps. The same seven-centavos stamp on the bottom could not be anything but a forgery, because it is so badly made. Look at the difference between the two heads!

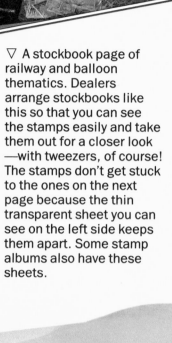

▽ A stockbook page of railway and balloon thematics. Dealers arrange stockbooks like this so that you can see the stamps easily and take them out for a closer look —with tweezers, of course! The stamps don't get stuck to the ones on the next page because the thin transparent sheet you can see on the left side keeps them apart. Some stamp albums also have these sheets.

△ A display stand in a stamp shop. These stands protect stamps and covers behind plastic sheets, but also let collectors see them easily and clearly.

◁ Choosing first day covers from a box on a stamp shop counter.

STAMP SHOPS AND FAIRS

△ The collector in the top picture chooses stamps from a stockbook. He has his tweezers ready to take out stamps he wants. The woman behind him is buying banknotes. Many stamp shops sell other things people collect, such as banknotes, coins or cigarette cards (small illustrated cards that were once given away in cigarette packs). The photograph in the bottom picture gives you some idea of the huge numbers of stamps a shop will stock. Look at the albums and filing boxes behind the dealers and at the back!

▷ Most stamp fairs are held indoors, but this one, in Paris, is open-air. Amsterdam, the Dutch capital, also has a regular fair like this. Open-air fairs are fun in summer when the weather's good, but not so enjoyable when it's raining or very windy!

Going into a stamp shop or fair is rather like entering Aladdin's treasure cave. Everywhere you look there are stamps—in albums, in stockbooks, on pages, on stands, in boxes or safely under glass if they are very valuable. Stamp dealers spend a great deal of time setting out their stocks of stamps and pricing them. Although the thousands of stamps may bewilder you at first, a dealer knows exactly where to find any stamp you ask for.

The big difference between shops and fairs is that shops open every day, but fairs take place only once a month or in some cases once a week. Dealers at fairs set up their stocks on tables that they pack away when the fair is over. The next week or month, they may be somewhere else. You need to know when and where a fair takes place—if you miss it, you'll have to wait a long time before it comes back. Dealers at fairs may sell stamps at lower prices than shops but they usually have a much smaller stock of stamps.

Buying stamps at auctions is very different from buying in shops or at fairs. An auction catalog shows you what is for sale, with an estimate of how much each "lot" is likely to cost. (A lot can be a single stamp or a whole collection.) People at auctions "bid," or say how much they want to pay for a lot. After each bid everyone else has a chance to bid a higher price. This goes on until nobody will bid any more. Whoever made the last highest bid gets the lot.

BUYING STAMPS BY MAIL

Many collectors buy stamps by mail. This may be because they live too far away from shops or stamp fairs or because they specialize in stamps that can only be bought from foreign countries. Collectors often prefer to buy at home because it gives them more time to decide what they want. Stamp dealers often prefer to sell by mail because it can save them the expense of running a shop or the effort of taking heavy loads of stamps to stamp fairs.

One way to buy stamps by mail is from "approval" books. These books fit into an ordinary envelope and contain pages of stamps with prices written next to them. You simply remove the stamps you want and return the book with your payment. You can usually find an approval book to suit your pocket and stamp interests.

Kiloware is sold by mail, though you usually pay for it in advance and you can't return what you don't want. Kiloware is the name for stamps on paper (bits of envelope or card) that are sold by weight, ranging from small bags to large sacks. You'll have lots of fun sorting through stamps from a kiloware bag and soaking them off the paper. It's also a very inexpensive way to buy stamps and find interesting postmarks from other countries.

HOW TO REMOVE STAMPS FROM PAPER

1 There are two ways to soak stamps off white, cream or light blue paper—that is, paper without a bright color that can run off in water. The first way is to put the paper in warm water with the stamps *face down*. Wait about 30 minutes till the stamps float free. Remove paper and stamps from the water, one at a time. Always handle wet stamps gently or they may tear.

2 The second way to soak off stamps is to place the paper in warm water *face up*. Leave it for 30 minutes. Now very gently push the stamps with your finger to see if they have come away from the paper. Remember that wet stamps can tear very easily. Even if a small part of the stamp is still stuck to the paper, leave it until it floats free by itself.

3 Here is a quick way to remove stamps from stripe-edged airmail envelopes or brightly colored paper, so that the colors don't run and stain the stamps. Use a shallow tray, *hot* water and a special stamp-removing liquid—you can also use ordinary liquid detergent. The stamps should float off almost at once. Take them out of the water quickly.

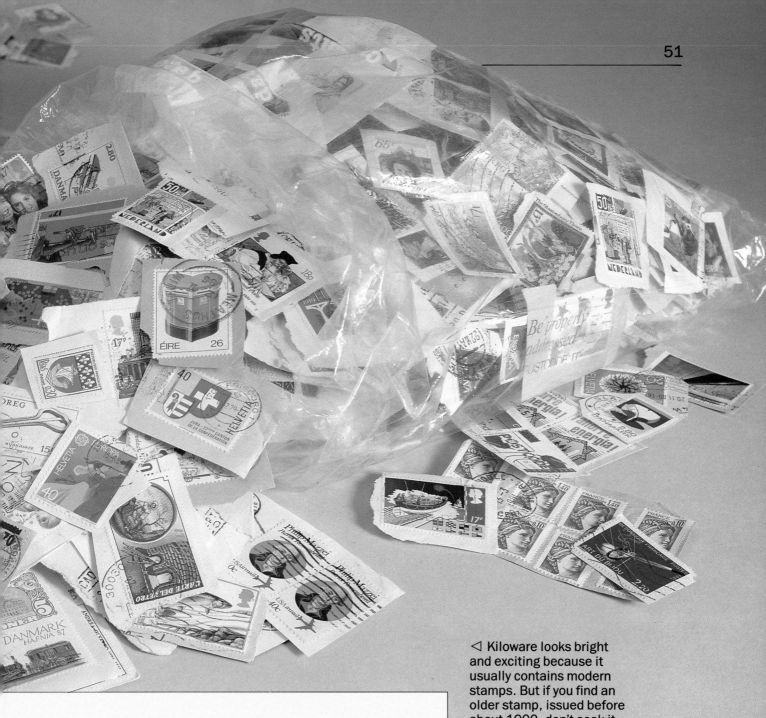

◁ Kiloware looks bright and exciting because it usually contains modern stamps. But if you find an older stamp, issued before about 1900, don't soak it off with the rest. Some older stamps have "fugitive" ink, which means the ink can run, or dissolve, in water. Instead, leave the stamp on paper and trim around it carefully with scissors.

4 Even after floating off in water, stamps may still have glue on the back. It looks like a grayish jelly. To get rid of it, run the back of the stamp under cold or slightly warm tap water. Hold the stamp gently but firmly between the underside of your thumb and a finger. Don't let the tap run too fast or the water may wash the stamp out of your hand.

5 To dry stamps, lay them on a sheet of white paper and let them dry for 15 minutes. Put the stamps between two *clean* sheets of blotting paper. Put the sheets inside the pages of a heavy book. Make sure the stamps are flat before you shut the book, or they may crease. If any stamps stick to the paper after drying, *don't* pull them off, but put them back in the water.

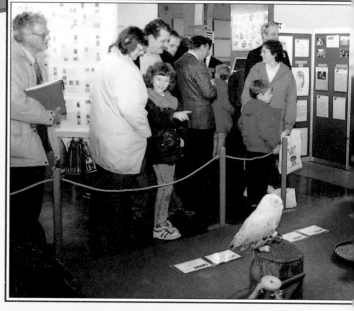

◁ Club members who want to sell stamps to other members send them out in books. About ten different books are sent out together in a "packet." This is a page from a book. Buyers remove what they want and make notes of what they have bought in the books. They send the money back to the Packet Secretary, who keeps track of all the books and money. The buyer then sends the packet to the next member on the list.

△ A collector checks a stamp display against his exhibition catalog. Exhibitions like this often take place at big stamp fairs that are held once or twice a year and are attended by hundreds of dealers and thousands of collectors from all over the country.

△ Big exhibitions usually have many fascinating displays. These collectors are admiring a live owl, the same bird that was shown on one of the stamps in a 1986 Europa nature conservation set. In front of the owl, you can just see a first day cover for the stamp. Behind the collectors is a display of bird thematics and one showing how the stamps were designed and printed.

CLUBS AND EXHIBITIONS

A t a stamp club, or philatelic society, as it is often called, everyone and everything to do with the stamp world come together. Club members chat about stamps and exchange information. Collectors give talks about stamps and show displays, or members may be invited to visit another club. Once or twice a year members take part in competitions and exhibitions, when they show pages from their collections on big boards and judges decide which displays are the best and most interesting.

Your school may already run a stamp club. If a club has enough young members it may run a "junior night" but if you can't find a local club to join, you could get together with some friends and start your own at school.

You can learn a great deal about stamps through a club; other collectors will want to share their enthusiasm and learn about your interests. No one minds if you are young or a new collector. All that matters is your interest in stamps.

Clubs are good places to buy and sell stamps. As well as stamp fairs, there are "bring and buy" evenings, where members buy and sell stamps. Clubs also run auctions, usually two or three times a year. Club circuit books, also called "the packet," are like approval books sent out by dealers in the mail (page 50). Any member can make up a book to be sent around to other members. You remove the stamps you want to buy and write your name in the space left by the stamp.

△ Here are two souvenir sheets printed for big exhibitions. The sheet for the 1965 Congress of the ISCA (**1**) celebrates the centenary of the post at Champéry, Switzerland. In the center is a picture of the first perforated Swiss stamp design of 1882. The other sheet (**2**) was issued to mark the twelfth anniversary in 1944 of the Bronx County Stamp Club of New York. In 1944, though, the United States was at war. So the sheet was overprinted with "BUY WAR BONDS" (buying War Bonds was a way people could help the government pay for the war). At the four corners of the sheet you can see pictures of wartime U.S. stamps.

CATALOGS

Since 1840 millions of stamps have been issued all over the world. A catalog will help you sort out and identify any one of these millions of stamps. Catalogs tell you how many stamps there are in a set, what their values are, when they were issued and what their subjects are. Stamps are printed in the language and alphabet of their country and have values shown in the country's own currency (money). A catalog explains all this clearly and simply.

Catalogs vary from very simple ones that list a stamp only once, to more specialized ones listing many variations of the same stamp design. They all list stamps in the order they were issued, with headings to show why commemoratives were printed.

Catalogs usually show pictures of stamps, often in color, and may also show watermarks or enlargements of parts of stamps to show printing varieties or errors. Most countries print special catalogs for their own stamps as well as ones for other countries. Other catalogs might list only first day covers or thematics. So, with the right catalog for the stamps you collect, you'll never get lost in the world of stamps.

▽ You can get a catalog of stamps for whatever country you collect. The same is true of the more popular thematic subjects. You can usually choose between simple catalogs or more specialized ones.

1 World—very simple
2 Great Britain and British Commonwealth—specialized
3 Great Britain—simple
4 Mammals—thematic, all world
5 Sports—thematic, all world
6 Belgium/Europa—specialized
7 France—specialized
8 This very specialized catalog lists the many variations of the French "Marianne" design stamps.
9 A supplement to update earlier catalogs with new issues. It saves buying a complete new catalog.
10 Germany—simple
11 United Nations—simple
12 The Netherlands and colonies —simple
13 U.S.A.—simple
14 U.S.A. first day covers
15 Canada—first day covers
16 Australia—simple
17 Communist China—simple
18 Belgium—specialized
19 Denmark—specialized
20 Faroe Islands—specialized
21 Austria—specialized

We have reproduced here a page from Scott's *Standard Postage Stamp Catalogue*, Volume 1, which shows an enlarged listing for a King George VI and Leopard stamp and a King George VI stamp. Parts of the listing are numbered and labeled to help you understand how to read a listing.

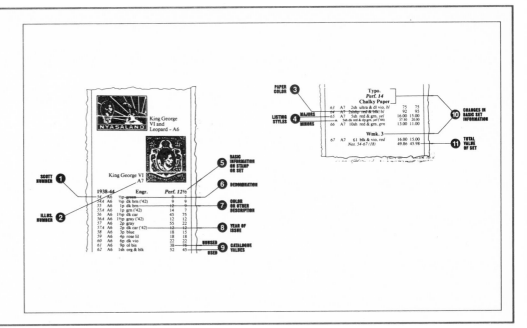

FAMOUS STAMPS

◁ This Guyana "stamp-on-stamp" costs a few cents and shows the world's most famous stamp, the 1856 British Guiana one-cent magenta (red). There is only one copy of the real stamp in the world and if sold it might cost well over a million dollars!

△ Mauritius, an Indian Ocean island, was the first British colony to issue stamps, in 1847. Stamps were ordered from Britain but they did not turn up in time. So, a local firm quickly printed some penny reds and twopenny blues, copied from the same value British stamps. Only 500 of each were printed, one at a time from an engraved plate. The stamps soon sold out and today "Post Office Mauritius" stamps are extemely rare.

△ The beautiful British £1 stamp for the 1929 Postal Union Congress (PUC) is one of Britain's most dramatic stamps. It shows the legend of St. George, patron saint of England, killing a dragon. Until 1980 the £1 PUC was the largest British stamp ever issued.

MAFEKING SIEGE STAMPS

△ In 1900, during the Boer war in southern Africa, the town of Mafeking was besieged for seven months by Dutch Boer settlers fighting their hated British rulers. This cigarette card shows a scene from the fighting and two stamps printed by the British forces trapped by the Boers. One stamp shows a soldier on a bicycle, the other shows Robert Stephenson Smyth Baden-Powell, hero of the siege and, later, founder of the Boy Scouts in 1908.

◁ A black swan was the badge of Western Australia and appeared on all the colony's stamps until 1902. The first "swan" stamp, the famous one-penny black, was issued in 1854 and is shown here on a 1985 Italian stamp issued for a stamp exhibition.

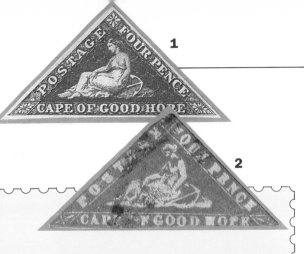

△ The beautifully engraved Cape of Good Hope four-penny blue triangular (**1**) was printed in Britain. When the stamps ran out, copies were made in the south African colony (**2**). They looked so rough, they were nicknamed "woodblocks," as if they had been printed from wood blocks. This rare stamp was printed in the wrong color, the red of the one-penny stamps, instead of blue.

◁ The famous 1851 "Hawaiian Missionary" stamps got their nickname because missionaries, who encouraged people to become Christians, used them when they worked in Hawaii and wrote back to the U.S. They are very rare now and even a century ago were prized by collectors—it was for one of these stamps that Gaston Leroux was murdered.

▽ These 1849 French one-franc rose stamps are two of the world's rarest stamps. They are joined as a *tête bêche* pair. Only one pair like it is known to exist. *Tête bêche* happens when one stamp printing plate is inverted so that a stamp is printed upside down next to another printed right side up.

Some stamps become famous because they are very rare and very valuable. Others are famous because collectors admire their beauty. Printing errors can add to a stamp's fame, as can a fascinating story behind a stamp's issue. Other stamps are famous simply because they are the first of their kind, like the 1850/51 "cotton-reels" of British Guiana. They were the first round stamps and got their nickname because they looked like labels on the ends of cotton-reels. The famous 1863 Cape of Good Hope triangulars were also the first stamps of their shape.

Some other unusual stamps, from Uganda, were made by a British missionary, the Reverend Millar, in 1895 and 1896. He printed each stamp on his typewriter and each stamp had its value in cowrie shells, which were what local people used instead of money. These stamps are known as "cowries."

Unfortunately, only rich people can afford most of these famous early stamps. But you can still collect them because many have been issued as "stamps-on-stamps," or illustrations of the originals on inexpensive modern stamps. Japanese "dragons," Swiss "cantonals" and Brazilian "bulls' eyes" are just a few of the famous old stamps issued as stamp-on-stamp thematics. Often they come from the same countries that issued the original stamps but sometimes they are commemorated by completely different countries.

◁ Brazil's first stamps, issued in 1843, were called "bulls' eyes" because the large egg-shaped design reminded people of huge eyes. There were three values, the 30 reis shown here, and 60 and 90 reis values, all printed black without a country name.

▷ This 1918 U.S. stamp is famous for two reasons. First, the Curtiss "Jenny" biplane in the center is upside down, which makes it a very valuable and rare error. Second, the stamp was the first of many U.S. airmail stamps.

AIRMAILS

THE SIEGE OF PARIS

In 1870 Gibson Bowles, an American reporter, was trapped in Paris when it was surrounded by the German Army in the Franco-Prussian War. He had to get stories of the siege out to his newspaper, so he had the idea of sending them by balloon. Balloons had carried mail before, but Bowles suggested a *regular* air service. The first Paris mail balloon, *Le Neptune*, left on September 23, with over a hundred kilos of mail, and landed a hundred kilometers away at Craconville. During the siege 65 balloons flew from the city, each one with some carrier pigeons, which were used to send replies back to Paris.

△ A mail balloon takes off from a makeshift army camp in Paris, when the city was surrounded by the German Army (**1**). It carried letters like the one below (**2**), which was sent out of Paris on November 5th, 1870. The siege lasted from September 1870 to January 1871. In the end the starving Parisians were forced to surrender. The 1971 French stamp (**3**) commemorates the centenary of the balloon post from the besieged city.

◁ Air letters such as these two from Great Britain are made of special light paper so that they weigh very little, allowing many of them to be carried by air at the same time. The first pre-stamped air letters like this were issued in Iraq in 1933.

◁ Air travel and airmail are especially important in countries such as Mexico, Peru, Brazil and the U.S. where distances are very great and land travel can be difficult. These airmail stamps are from Mexico, one of several countries that issue special stamps for letters carried by plane.

▽ In 1919 Henry Hawker and K. Mackenzie Grieve took off from Newfoundland, Canada, to cross the Atlantic to England. But, as the cigarette card picture shows, (**1**) they crashed into the sea, just 2,400 kilometers out. The cover (**2**) was on board the plane and is what collectors call "crash mail." The specially overprinted three-cent brown stamp almost floated off but was recovered from the water and was stuck back on.

1

2

Airmail, or sending letters by air transport, began with balloon mail, many years before the first engine-powered aircraft flew in 1903. But early balloons were carried to their destination by the wind, which might blow in the wrong direction or might not blow at all! It was not until there were reliable planes that it was possible to be sure letters would arrive at a certain destination at a certain time.

The first official airmail flight was in India in February 1911. Later that year flights were made in Britain, Denmark, Italy and the U.S. In 1917, during World War I, the Italians ran airmail services between Rome and Turin. Another service, between Rome and Naples, used seaplanes, which could land on water. These were used instead of ships, which were in danger from enemy submarines.

Airmail is very important in North and South American countries, where mail travels huge distances or where land travel is very difficult. U.S. airmail services began in 1918 with a flight between Washington, D.C., New York and Philadelphia. Stamps issued for this flight were the first of many famous U.S. airmail stamps.

▽ The giant Zeppelin airships were named after their German inventor, Count von Zeppelin. The biplane (two-winged) aircraft seen with a Zeppelin on this postcard (**1**) was at first a less efficient way to fly. Zeppelins regularly flew passengers and mail across the Atlantic long before aircraft did. In the 1930s many countries issued stamps to commemorate Zeppelin flights, including this 1930 U.S. stamp (**2**).

2

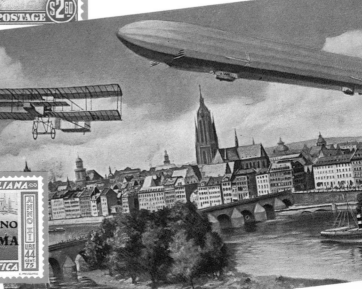

1

▽ Italian pilots were great pioneers of long, often risky flights. These three 1933 Italian stamps commemorate a transatlantic flight by a huge formation of Italian planes from Rome, Italy's capital. The stamps were overprinted *Volo di Ritorno* ("return flight") for the journey back from New York, but were never used on letters.

ODD MAILS

△ The Tonga Tin Can Mail began in 1882 after a shark killed a swimmer carrying letters out to a ship. The mail was sealed into tin cans and carried out by boat instead. You can see this on this stamp from a 1982 set celebrating the Tin Can Mail centenary.

Delivering mail has not always been as simple as just pushing letters through front-door mailboxes. Letters have been sent, for instance, by pneumatic post. Used for short distances in large cities, pneumatic post was a system in which mail was put into special containers that were propelled, or pushed, at high speed by air pressure through underground tubes. Great Britain had a pneumatic post service in 1859, but it was not successful. Later France, Germany, Austria and Italy used better pneumatic post systems.

Some very unusual ways of delivering mail have been used on land that is difficult for wheeled vehicles to travel over. For example, llamas have carried mail in Bolivia, where there are few good roads on the steep slopes of South America's Andes Mountains. Camels, which can for days go without water, have been used in the vast deserts of Egypt and the Sudan. Russian mail was often taken across thick winter snows by troika sleighs pulled by reindeer or horses. Reindeer were also used in parts of Scandinavia.

Jagged coral reefs, rocky coasts or strong sea currents make it very dangerous for ships to come close to small islands without proper harbors. Putting mail in floating barrels, biscuit tins, tin cans or bottles are just a few methods that have been used to get mail from ship to shore and back again on such islands.

All these odd methods show how important the mail is. Whatever the difficulty, even in very dangerous wartime conditions, the mail somehow reaches its destination.

△ This French stamp shows a post office on a dangerous, muddy battlefield of World War I (1914-18). It was a Field Post Office for soldiers' mail. You can see the postmaster poking his head through the window of the tiny shed. The sign below him tells soldiers that he was there on Mondays and Fridays. The sign to his left says "Pay-desk, please knock," and the sign below it reads "letterbox."

◁ It was unsafe for sailing ships to get too close to Pacific islands like Samoa, Tonga or the Solomons. But flat-bottomed craft could safely sail over any rocks or shallow water. This Samoan stamp shows mail being carried on a raft.

△ This special Italian pneumatic post stamp was issued in 1924. It is similar to a definitive stamp design of 1906, showing King Victor Emmanuel III, but it is wider so that it can carry the words *Posta Pneumatica*, or pneumatic post. The stamp's original value was 15 centesimi but this has been overprinted for a new 20 centismi value.

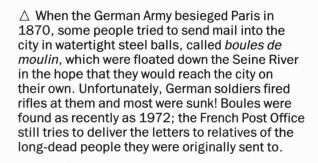

△ When the German Army besieged Paris in 1870, some people tried to send mail into the city in watertight steel balls, called *boules de moulin*, which were floated down the Seine River in the hope that they would reach the city on their own. Unfortunately, German soldiers fired rifles at them and most were sunk! Boules were found as recently as 1972; the French Post Office still tries to deliver the letters to relatives of the long-dead people they were originally sent to.

▽ The German mailman in this picture provides a complete postal service for his customers. He carries a tray of postcards and stamps to sell to people in an open-air restaurant, who then write messages to friends and put the postcards in the letter box the mailman carries on his back.

▽ This special mailman's cycle was called a "hen and chicken" cycle. Its five wheels made it steadier to ride with a heavy bag of mail than ordinary bicycles.

▽ Pigeons have a wonderful sense of direction and can be trained to fly away and return to the same place. This makes them very useful for carrying messages or letters. Pigeon posts were used in the Netherlands as long ago as 1575. This picture shows French army post pigeons setting out on their journeys.

STAMPS GO TO WAR

Stamps and letters can lead dangerous lives. They have taken part in revolutions, invasions and wars, and when the fighting ends, stamps may be used to remember these events. For example, many stamps of France and Russia commemorate the battles, sieges and other terrible events these countries experienced in World War II.

Stamps even helped *cause* a war when South American neighbors, Bolivia and Paraguay, both claimed the same area of land and both issued stamps with maps showing the Gran Chaco region as their own!

Revolutionaries who overthrow their governments often issue their own stamps. This is what Mexican revolutionaries did in 1914, as did the Russian revolutionaries after 1917, and, more recently, those who toppled the Shah of Iran in 1979.

Countries at war often issued special stamps for other countries they conquered. This is why German stamps were overprinted with the names of Bulgaria and Rumania, which Germany occupied in World War I.

In wartime, mail is usually censored, and letters are opened by officials who check that writers do not give away any secrets; for example, a soldier overseas may mention where his unit is. The enemy must not know this, so the censor obliterates or cuts out the information. The letter is then sent on, marked to show that the censor has read it.

Wars end and the fighting stops. Soldiers go home and peace returns. But censored letters, "occupation" stamps and other stamps at war are still around today to remind us of the horrors of war.

▷ The U.S. did not enter World War I against Germany until 1917, after some Americans were drowned when a German submarine sank the British liner *Lusitania*, shown here on an Isle of Man stamp.

△ In World War II most of Europe was invaded by Nazi Germany. Norway was occupied in 1940, but the king and his government escaped to freedom and exile in Britain, where they issued their own "exile" stamps. This one shows a road on which is written, in Norwegian, "We Will Win."

▷ This Polish stamp shows *Orzel*, a submarine that sailed to England to escape the Nazis when they invaded Poland in World War II. The stamp is one of a set issued in 1970 showing Polish ships that, like *Orzel*, fought in the war.

◁ This beautiful stamp is not a postage stamp; it is an example of a "Cinderella" stamp, or label printed to look like a stamp. This French one was issued during World War I (1914–1918). It was sold to people who wanted to be patriotic by sticking the stamp on letters alongside real stamps.

▷ Every war has its sad victims. The 1987 British stamp (**1**) shows a nurse helping a man injured by World War II bombs. The 1946 Austrian "charity" stamp (**2**) shows a prisoner of war. The "+2" by the 8g value shows that for each stamp sold, two groschen were given to aid prisoners.

▽ Germany conquered France in 1940. General de Gaulle, leader of the Free French forces, who was exiled in England, encouraged the French not to give up with a message that began: "France has lost a battle! But France has not lost the War!" By 1944 France was liberated, and this French stamp celebrates the 20th anniversary of the event by printing the famous message of 1940.

△ This 1973 block of four U.S. stamps is a "composite." Each stamp makes a picture on its own, but together they form a larger picture that shows the Boston Tea Party, an incident that helped cause the American War of Independence from British rule. In 1773 American colonists, dressed as Indians, boarded a British ship in Boston harbor and threw its cargo of tea chests into the water (you can see the splash of the boxes in the bottom left of the stamp). It was a protest against a tea tax the British made the Americans pay.

STAMPS WITH MESSAGES

Stamps can carry important messages. A red cross on a stamp is usually to remind people of the Red Cross, an organization that helps prisoners of war or people who suffer in disasters such as floods. France regularly issues Red Cross Fund stamps. They have two values on them—one for the postage and one to help pay for Red Cross work. New Zealand Health stamps also carry an extra charge to help pay for children's health camps.

Some stamps tell of disasters or warn of disasters that may happen if nothing is done to stop them. For example, some years ago, people were worried that Venice, an Italian city built on islands in the sea, was sinking. Stamps were issued to help the work of saving the city. In 1961 an earthquake on the Atlantic island of Tristan da Cunha forced all the islanders to leave. When they returned, two years later, the island issued stamps to help pay for rebuilding.

Propaganda stamps are sometimes issued to try and change people's minds about politics. Both sides in World War II did this. For example, in 1943, leaders of Britain, the U.S. and Russia met in Teheran, Iran, to find a way to work together to beat Germany and win the war. The Germans printed some stamp forgeries that attempted to trick British people into losing confidence in their leaders by making them think the meeting in Teheran was an awful mistake.

△ This Danish stamp shows the name of the worldwide Red Cross Organization, which was started in 1863, in 31 different languages. In Muslim countries, the organization is called the Red Crescent, which you can see in the bottom left corner of the stamp. The lion was the sign of the Red Cross in Iran until 1979.

▷ Sadly, many people are killed or injured in road accidents. These stamps encourage road safety. The West German issue (**1**) warns against drinking alcohol and driving. The Italian stamp (**2**) simply shows the result of bad driving. The Dutch stamp (**3**) reminds drivers to watch out for children crossing roads.

▷ These beautiful *se-tenant* (joined) stamps celebrate Christmas and come from an island named after the holiday. Christmas Island got its name because a British explorer, James Cook, discovered it on Christmas Day, 1771. Other stamps with greetings messages are the "love" stamps issued by Ireland and the U.S. for Valentine's day.

▽ The Netherlands issued this stamp showing pages from a pop-up book in its 1980 Child Welfare set.

▷ These French and Italian stamps warn against the dangers of smoking. Many countries issue antismoking stamps. Some are quite frightening and show skulls or skeletons.

◁ Crime is a problem everywhere. Unfortunately, there are not enough police to catch all the criminals. This U.S. stamp encourages Americans to help the police by watching for suspicious-looking people who might be breaking the law.

▷ These stamps show how Hitler tried to stop Russia and Britain from fighting together against Germany in World War II. The top stamp is a real British stamp issued when George VI was crowned king in 1937. It shows him with his wife Queen Elizabeth. Hitler thought that Stalin, Russia's leader, would invade Britain and Europe if Germany lost the war and stopped fighting Russia. So, Germany issued a propaganda forgery of the 1937 stamp, showing Stalin instead of Elizabeth. It was meant to scare the British into thinking they would be ruled by Stalin if they helped him beat Germany.

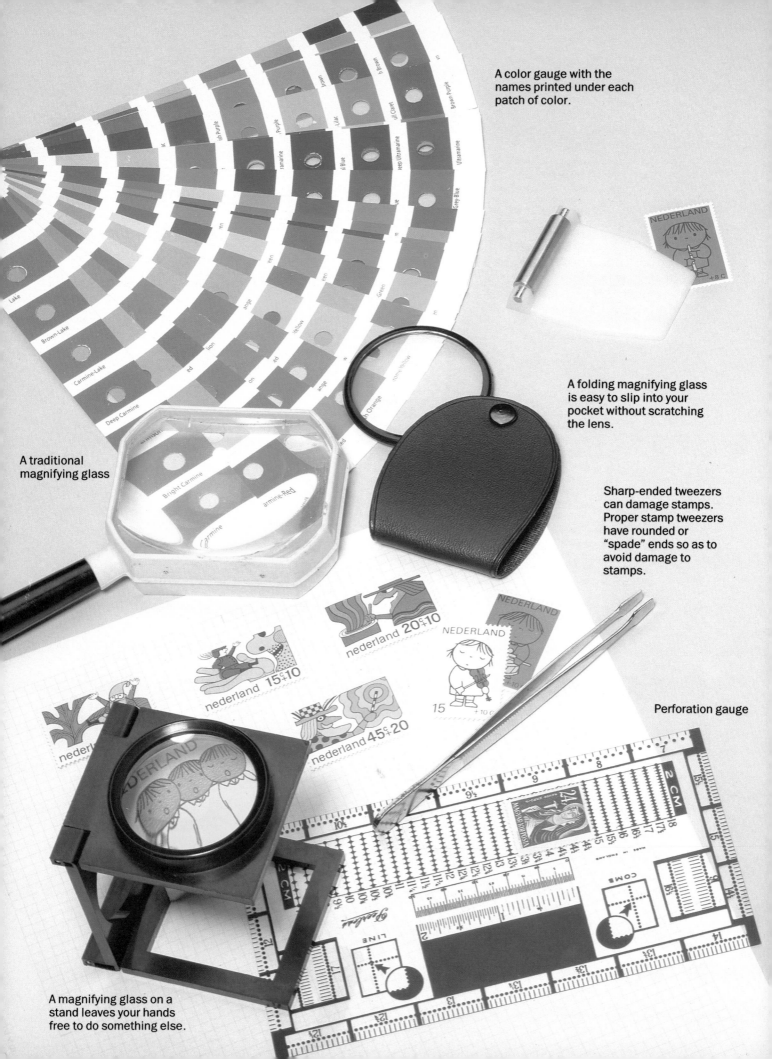

A color gauge with the names printed under each patch of color.

A folding magnifying glass is easy to slip into your pocket without scratching the lens.

A traditional magnifying glass

Sharp-ended tweezers can damage stamps. Proper stamp tweezers have rounded or "spade" ends so as to avoid damage to stamps.

Perforation gauge

A magnifying glass on a stand leaves your hands free to do something else.

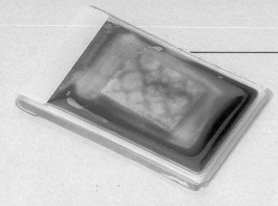

THE TOOLS OF COLLECTING

△ This watermark detector has a small plastic bag filled with a special blue liquid. You put the stamp face-down under the bag and pull the roller across to spread the liquid thinly over the stamp. As if by magic, you'll see the pattern of the watermark appear.

▽ A watermark seen against black paper.

△ This 1964 stamp, issued for the 25th anniversary of Denmark's Stamp Day, shows perforation and watermark varieties.

◁ Perforations are measured by the number of holes there are every two centimeters. Several types of perforation gauges are available, but all are fairly similar. This one has all the different "perfs" printed as black dots on clear plastic. You place the stamp on top of the gauge and match the dots to the perfs. This Hungarian stamp is perf 15, or 15 holes every two centimeters.

You need to look after your stamps. You may want to know the exact color shade of a stamp or the size of its perforations. You may even want to identify the watermark hidden in the paper of a stamp. To do all this you need some special tools.

Perforations are holes punched around a stamp so you can remove it from a sheet without damaging it. Some holes are bigger than others, and the same stamp design may be issued with different-sized perforations. You can check the hole size on a perforation gauge.

A catalog may say that two color variations of the same stamp are "red-orange" or "orange-red." What's the difference? One is more orangey, the other is redder. Find out which is which by matching the stamp against small color patches on a color gauge. One stamp could be much more valuable than the other.

Some stamps have watermarks, or patterns *in* the paper, not the printing. The pattern is formed when the paper is made. Where the watermark appears, the paper is very slightly thinner than the rest of the paper. You can see this quite clearly by holding plain paper up to the light. Unfortunately, the printing on a stamp hides the watermark. One way to detect a watermark is to place the stamp face down on black paper. The black paper will usually show through the thinner paper, revealing the watermark pattern. If this does not work, you may find a simple watermark detector useful.

If you want to see the tiny details of stamps, you'll need a magnifying glass. There are several types and you should choose whichever suits you best.

The most important tool of all is a pair of tweezers to pick up stamps. If you use fingers to pick up stamps you may make them grubby or damage the fragile perforations. You can spoil the gum on a mint stamp because no matter how dry your hands seem, there's always a bit of sweat left: dampness is the sworn enemy of gum!

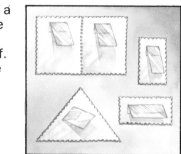

HOW TO MOUNT STAMPS

1 Before you mount a stamp, work out exactly where it goes. Now fold the hinge about a third of the way down to give a short edge and a long flap. You can also buy ready-folded hinges.

2 Lay the stamp face down. Slightly wet the small edge of the hinge. Fix it to the back of the stamp, as near to the top of the stamp as possible, but so none of the hinge shows from the front.

3 Now wet only the bottom part of the longer hinge flap. Don't wet it too much or wet the stamp because you may stick the stamp to the page. Always use tweezers for safety's sake.

4 Carefully position the stamp on the page. You should know exactly where it goes but if you make a mistake, let the hinge dry for ten minutes or more. It will peel off easily, with no damage to stamp or page.

5 Triangular stamps need a hinge in the middle or one on each side. For small stamps, cut hinges in half. With pairs or strips, hinge each stamp. Blocks need hinges near each corner.

6 Pocket mounts with transparent fronts let you stick mint stamps on a page without damaging the gum with a hinge. Just slip the stamp in the mount, moisten the back of the mount and stick it in.

HOW TO CARE FOR YOUR STAMPS

◁ This picture shows different sorts of albums. The peg-fitting (**1**), springback (**2**) and ringbinder (**3**) albums have loose leaves so that you can add extra pages as your collection grows. Some albums are made like books, so you need a new album when they're full up. This one has pictures of stamps beside spaces for the real stamps (**4**). Another drawback to this sort of album is that it has no room for things like covers, which you could mount on a plain page with photograph corners (normally used for photos in a snapshot album). If you collect lots of first day covers you'll need an album with clear pockets for the covers (**5**). As well as hinges (**6**), you may need some transparent 'pocket' mounts for mint stamps (**7**).

Stamps are pieces of paper. Paper tears easily and can get stained and dirty. Damp will spoil the gum on a mint stamp. If you want your stamps looking their best, handle them carefully and look after them.

Work on a clean, dry table top — stamps can easily pick up dirt or damp. Don't have food or drink on the table — cola or tea, for example, could ruin a stamp.

You need an album to display and protect your stamps. There are many different types and you should choose whichever suits you. A stock book (see page 48) is useful because instead of sticking stamps onto its pages, you slip them into long pockets. This is a neat way to store stamps you've not yet arranged. But be careful when you slip a stamp into a pocket, or you may damage the perforations. It's a good idea, too, to move mint stamps in the pockets from time to time. If left too long, the gum may stick to the stockbook pages.

Always keep albums and stockbooks in a dry place. If damp gets in, your stamps may become 'foxed' with rust-coloured marks that are difficult to remove. It's best to stick your stamps on only one side of a page of a stockbook or album. Stamps placed on both sides easily get entangled and damaged. Some albums have thin, clear sheets between each page to stop this happening.

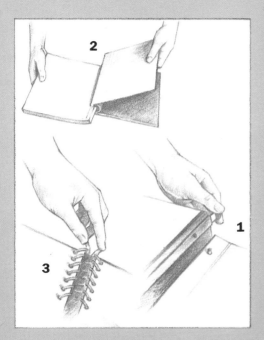

◁ When you add a page to a peg-binder album (**1**) you must remove all the pages that come before the new one. Peg-binders can be a bit fiddly but they hold the pages firmly, with little danger of tearing the holes. A spring-back album (**2**) is fairly cheap to buy and has a strong spring to grip the pages. They don't lie flat, so you need to remove a page to add stamps to it. You must remove *all* the pages to add a new page. Ring-binder albums (**3**) allow you to add pages without removing any others. The holes on the pages should be strengthened with little cloth rings to stop them tearing. 'Multiring' binders have about 20 rings and there is less danger of tearing the holes.

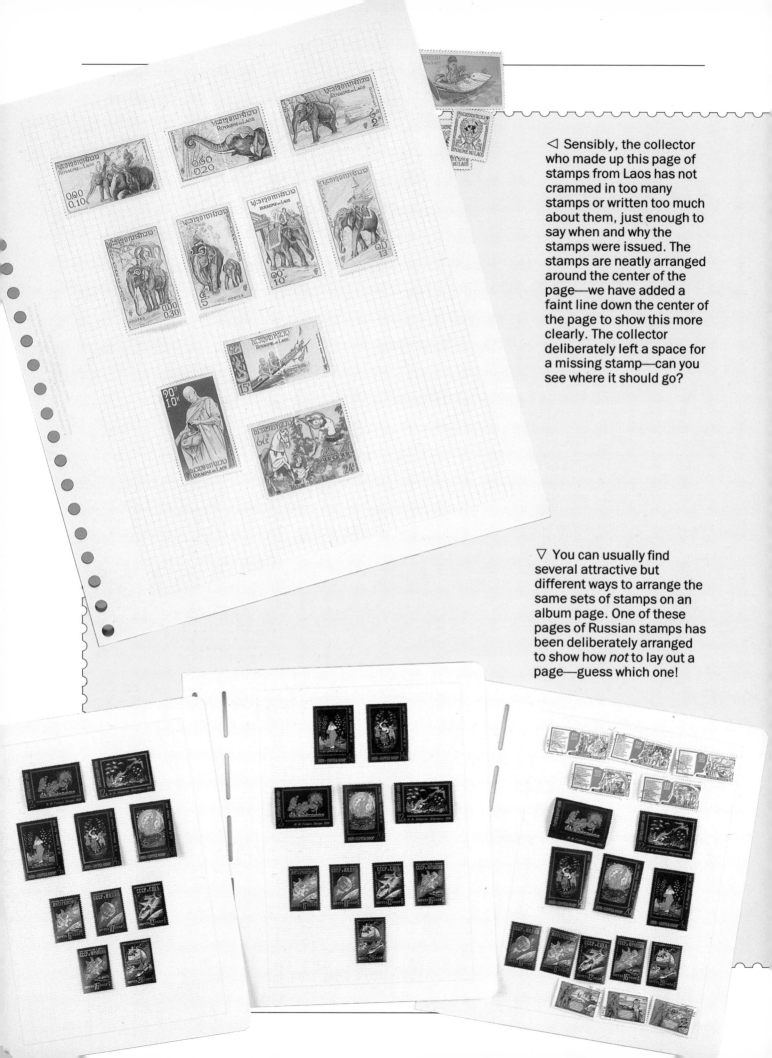

◁ Sensibly, the collector who made up this page of stamps from Laos has not crammed in too many stamps or written too much about them, just enough to say when and why the stamps were issued. The stamps are neatly arranged around the center of the page—we have added a faint line down the center of the page to show this more clearly. The collector deliberately left a space for a missing stamp—can you see where it should go?

▽ You can usually find several attractive but different ways to arrange the same sets of stamps on an album page. One of these pages of Russian stamps has been deliberately arranged to show how *not* to lay out a page—guess which one!

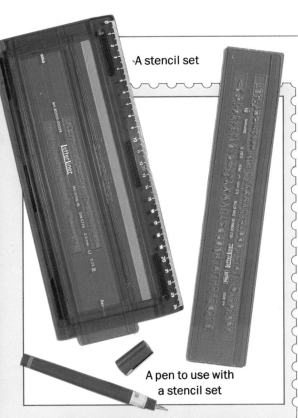

A stencil set

A pen to use with
a stencil set

△ Stencil sets are not expensive and usually provide different sizes of letters—small ones to write up the actual stamps and larger ones for page headings. This stencil slides backward and forward on a support, which makes it easy to write in straight lines.

▷ These are a few of the ways you can write up a collection. A stencil and special pen give very neat results (**1**), though it's a slow method and can be messy if you're not very careful. If you can use an italic pen, italic writing can be beautiful (**2**). Some people prefer to write block letters freehand (**3**).

Ready-printed "country" labels are inexpensive and an easy way to head each page (**4**). Typed pages can look extremely professional, but it's hard to position everything accurately.

Choose a method you like and find easy to use to write up your collection.

HOW TO ARRANGE STAMPS

Your collection is a very personal thing that should please *you*. You'll enjoy it more if your stamps are neatly and attractively arranged. Your album page can help you here. When you buy an album, try to get one with pages printed on small, faint squares, marked or numbered, if possible, to show the center. This will make it much easier to arrange the stamps neatly around the center of the page.

Try different arrangements of loose stamps on the page. Don't try and cram in too many. When you find an arrangement you like, lightly mark the positions of the stamps with a soft pencil you can later erase.

Try to lay out stamps in the same order in which they were issued, starting with the lowest values and ending with the highest ones. Don't worry if you can't do this without making an ugly page—arrange the stamps in the order that *looks* best, keeping them as near as possible to their correct order.

A catalog will help you "write up" a page with information about the stamps, such as perforation sizes or issue dates. Don't write too much or you'll end up with more writing than stamps! Practice what you want to write on scrap paper so you know exactly how much space to allow for it on the page. To avoid damage, write up a page before you mount the stamps.

Arranging stamps takes time and patience, but it's worth it for a collection that you can be proud of, and it will give you hours of pleasure.

1 Stenciled writing

BEAUTIFUL STAMPS

2 Italic handwriting

Beautiful Stamps

3 Freehand block letters

BEAUTIFUL STAMPS

4 Ready-printed country label

INDIA

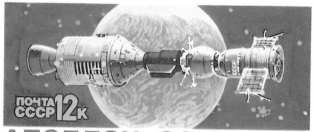

△ When the United States spacecraft Apollo linked up in space with the Russian spacecraft Soyuz in 1975, it was a very exciting achievement. It showed that the two great rivals in the world could cooperate with each other. The two countries had a stamp linkup too. They issued these pairs of stamps, using the same pictures of their crafts high above the earth's surface.

▽ In 1983 British Commonwealth countries got together to issue an omnibus for Commonwealth Day, March 14. Singapore's set showed the names of Commonwealth countries printed in a spiral around the logo, or symbol, of the Commonwealth.

△ Every spring, European countries get together to issue an omnibus of Europa stamps. The 1986 Europa theme was Nature Conservation. This is how Great Britain and France pictured the theme, Britain with a picture of a rare toad, France with a bat.

STAMP OMNIBUSES

The subjects shown on most stamps are chosen to tell people something about the countries that issue them. Some subjects, though, are of interest and importance to people all over the world. Occasionally several countries get together to issue stamps or sets of stamps about the same subject. Each country uses its own currency but the stamps may have a similar design. These stamps are called "omnibuses" and are usually issued by all the countries on the same day.

Aircraft, for example, are important everywhere. The 75th anniversary of the first powered aircraft, the Wright Brothers' "Flyer 1," was marked by omnibus issues from all over the world. Malaria is a terrible disease that affects people in tropical countries. "Malaria Eradication" was a 1962 omnibus to help the fight against the disease. Almost every country in the world competes in the Olympic Games, which take place every four years. This event always sees hundreds of sporting omnibuses.

Europa stamps are issued every year by a group of European countries. They are usually omnibuses but not always. For example, in 1986 most Europa countries issued stamps about wildlife, but Germany issued some stamps about sculpture.

Thematic collectors love omnibuses because they mean many stamps on one theme and all at the same time. Some omnibuses have special miniature sheets or booklets and, of course, first day covers.

△ Many countries issued stamps to commemorate 1979's International Year of the Child. Naturally, children or subjects that interest children were shown on most designs. One of Great Britain's stamps showed a scene from the famous children's story *Alice in Wonderland* (**1**). The Hungarian stamp shows a scene from another children's story, "Gallant John and the Dragons" (**2**). The Dutch stamp tells us that there are many children who need our help (**3**), while the Spanish stamp shows a child's painting of a library (**4**).

◁ The Olympic Games is the greatest international sports event in the world. Countries that send teams of athletes to the games issue an omnibus of stamps every time the games are held, that is every four years. These Belgian and U.S. stamps belong to the Olympics omnibus of 1984.

STAMP ERRORS

I f you find a fault in something you buy, you may throw it away or return it to the shop and complain. But collectors are thrilled to find stamps with printing mistakes that can make them more valuable than perfectly printed ones.

An "error" is usually an obvious mistake in a stamp such as the few stamps misprinted in a 1901 U.S. set for the Pan-American Exposition: three values, the one-, two- and three-cent, had inverted (upside-down) frames.

There are also design errors, when a designer or the people who choose a design make a mistake. For example, in 1956 East Germany printed some stamps to mark the centenary of the death of the composer Robert Schumann. The stamps showed Schumann and a sheet of his music. Unfortunately, thousands of stamps were printed showing music by a completely different composer, Franz Schubert!

Errors are often called varieties or flaws, which are usually small, often hard-to-see printing mistakes. They may happen when a printing machine doesn't work properly. If something hard or sharp, like a bit of grit or a piece of metal, scrapes against a printing plate it may damage it and leave a tiny line or dot that will show up when the stamp is printed. For example, a 1935 Maltese set of stamps showed a castle; a few stamps were printed with an extra line on one of the towers, which looked like an extra flagstaff. The extra flagstaff variety or flaw is about forty times more valuable than a normal one. Other varieties or flaws include different watermarks and different shades of the normal color.

△ In 1962 the United States commemorated Dag Hammarskjöld, the United Nations Secretary-General who died in 1961. The U.N. building in New York is on the left of the stamps. But on the bottom stamp, the yellow background was printed upside down. The top stamp is what collectors call a "normal." When this error was discovered, the U.S. Post Office printed thousands more of the yellow error to stop it from becoming rare and valuable.

▷ The overprint on this Finnish stamp is a hundred years too early. The flight of the Zeppelin airship that it commemorates was not made until 1930. The year 1830 overprinted in error on this stamp was eight years before the airship's inventor, Count von Zeppelin, was even born!

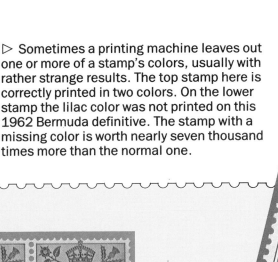

▷ Sometimes a printing machine leaves out one or more of a stamp's colors, usually with rather strange results. The top stamp here is correctly printed in two colors. On the lower stamp the lilac color was not printed on this 1962 Bermuda definitive. The stamp with a missing color is worth nearly seven thousand times more than the normal one.

◁ Something went wrong when this block of 1938 British fourpenny King George VI definitives was perforated. As you can see, some edges of the stamps were perforated, but others were not and came out imperforate, the collector's word for stamps with no perforations.

▽ St. Kitts-Nevis, a British colony in the Caribbean, issued this stamp in 1920. It has a design error. Christopher Columbus, the first European to sail to America, is shown on the right using a telescope, which was not invented until 1608, over a hundred years after Columbus died! It may have been the artist's fault or it may have been the fault of the people who asked the artist to design the stamp and told him to include a telescope.

THE BEAUTY OF STAMPS

Stamps are often called "art in miniature," and it certainly takes a variety of artistic skills to make a good stamp. First, it has to be designed. Then a photographer may take a picture for the stamp or an artist may do a painting for it. Recess-printed stamps need highly-talented engravers to "draw" designs onto metal plates. Colors have to be carefully chosen to make a stamp look its best. Finally, the stamp goes to the printer, where good or bad printing can improve or ruin a design.

But even if each job has been done well, people will still disagree about what is beautiful in a stamp and what is not, just as some people like the beauty of rugged mountains but others prefer gentler rolling hills covered with trees. Some collectors admire the simple beauty and gentle coloring of Swedish stamps, for example, while others prefer the brilliant colors of many modern stamps, such as Spanish ones. Plain white space around a design makes it stand out clearly, and collectors often feel this adds to a stamp's beauty.

For some people, the most beautiful stamp is the very first one, the Penny Black. Other collectors prefer later stamps with beautiful detailed frames, while most collectors agree that France has issued many beautiful engraved stamps.

You, too, will have your own favorites. Your friends may disagree with you and may prefer something else. This doesn't mean you are right and they are wrong or the other way around. What *is* important is to collect stamps you find attractive and that will please *you*.

▷ These stamps were issued in 1985 for the Europa Year of Music. All the stamps have the same theme, but each one has been designed completely differently. Which do you prefer? The bold Danish stamp (**1**) just shows some musical notes; the French stamp (**2**) shows a French monk, Adam de la Halle, writing music over 700 years ago; the Belgian stamp (**3**) shows two people cut out of a sheet of music and the British stamp (**4**), illustrates Gustav Holst's famous suite, "The Planets."

▷ This stamp comes from a long set of 23 issued by Austria in 1945. As you can see from the fine lines in the design, the stamp is engraved. Engraving, which is very skillful work, produces sharp, clear pictures and many collectors find these very attractive. The stamp also has beautiful borders on three of its sides.

◁ Not all modern stamps are brightly colored. This 1985 stamp shows how impressive a stamp can look in black and white. The stamp comes from the British Film Year set and shows the actor and comedian Peter Sellers.

▷ Jules Verne, a French author, wrote exciting adventure and science fiction stories. This stamp from Monaco captures the drama of one of his books. The swirling engraved lines seem to suggest the excitement you feel when you are caught up in a good adventure story.

◁ Paintings can make beautiful stamps and often appear on colorful thematic sets. France, for example, began a long series of sets of paintings in 1961. This 1969 stamp shows "The Circus," a painting by a famous French artist, Georges Seurat. The stamp comes from the corner of a sheet and has a special first day postmark in the margin.

◁ The circular date stamp, or "cds," as collectors call it, on this Swedish stamp is very simple. It shows just the town in Sweden the letter was mailed from and the date it was sent. Circular date stamp cancellations are much prized by collectors because they are so neat, clean and easy to read.

△ The lozenge-shaped postmark with bars and number was used a great deal in the U.S. forty or fifty years ago. This stamp comes from the Panama Canal Zone, which came under U.S. control in 1903 and issued its own stamps until 1979.

1

◁ "Save Nature and Animals" is the message on this slogan cancellation from Switzerland (**1**). It also shows the panda, which is the symbol of the World Wildlife Fund. Slogan postmarks are also issued by France, Britain and many other countries. They are an attractive way of giving information to the public. The cancellation on the 1977 Portuguese stamp (**2**) is a special first day postmark, with the same portrait on it as the stamp.

2

▽ The strange-looking gadget on this 1976 Italian stamp is an early franking or postmarking machine. Like modern machines used today, it was meant to save time when there were many letters to be posmarked. See if you can figure out how this machine operated.

▽ "Wavy-line" postmarks have been used for many years. This one comes from Sweden and has circular postmarks as well. The wavy lines do the same job as bar cancels: They make sure that all the stamps on an envelope are canceled and can't be used again.

△ With postmarks such as these bar cancels, no one can doubt that these Japanese stamps have been used! The U.S. also uses bar cancels made by machines that frank the stamps all at once. You often find them on large envelopes where the stamps are spread out.

△ This 1981 French "pre-cancel" stamp looks both mint *and* used! It has a printed cancel that is part of the stamp design. This saves time because letters can go straight through the mail without having to be franked first. A mint pre-cancel still has gum on the back. If there is no gum, it has been used and the stamp has been soaked off a cover after going through the mail.

▽ This Australian "Frama" label (**1**) was dispensed by a computerized machine that allowed people to buy stamps after the post office was closed. The Jersey meter cancel (**2**) was printed by a machine as the letter was passed through it. Meter canceling saves licking lots of stamps and stops people from stealing stamps from offices where they work.

POSTMARKS

Postmarks are used to mark or cancel stamps and show that they have been used. This, of course, is meant to stop people from using the stamps again and cheating the Post Office.

Postmarks on letters are usually circular. Other postmarks, or cancellations as they are often called, are large and oblong. They can be very black and heavy, like parcel postmarks. Some countries, such as the U.S. and Japan, use sets of long bars as cancellations.

The neatest postmarks are made by steel "cancelers." They may be made by machine or stamped by hand. If you see a very smudgy circular postmark, it has usually been made by a rubber hand-stamp. These tend to "slide" or slip on contact with an envelope.

Some postmarks have their own names. One is a "slogan" postmark, which has a printed message as well as the stamp cancellation. Another is a "killer" postmark, which is a very heavy postmark that is designed to cover as much as possible of a stamp with very thick black marks. There is also the "lozenge" postmark, shaped like a long oval filled with thick bars.

Most postmarks are black, but the Maltese Cross cancellation, used on the first British stamps, can also be found in red, blue, magenta (a bluish red) and even yellow. In October 1935 Czechoslovakia used red and blue postmarks as Independence Day souvenirs. There have even been postmarks in three colors, such as those used on letters posted at the Philympia stamp exhibition held in London in 1970.

1

2

CINDERELLAS

Stamps that are not stamps

Not all the stamps you see on sale are postage stamps. Some are "cinderellas," which look like postage stamps, with gum on their backs and perforated edges, but were issued for different reasons and cannot be used to pay postage. Few catalogs list cinderellas and for a long time collectors ignored them, treating them as worthless scraps of paper. Today, however, many people find them just as interesting as real stamps.

Cinderellas are printed to commemorate big exhibitions or to raise money for charities. Every Christmas, countries like the U.S. and Greenland issue special labels, which are stuck on Christmas card envelopes with real postage stamps. There are also cinderella labels for airmail, registered letters and parcel post.

You can also find "patriotic" labels that encourage people to support their country, particularly if it is fighting a war. Some places use cinderellas as advertisements, such as the tiny island of Herm, in the Channel Islands, near the French coast.

Other cinderellas are called "fiscals" and are used to pay tax or duty on goods or when a fee has to be paid to the government after a legal document is signed, such as the papers that prove that a person has sold his or her house to someone else. "Stamp Duty" is often printed on fiscals issued by English-speaking countries.

Cinderellas are usually easy to find and most are very inexpensive. They are interesting and attractive additions that will brighten up any stamp collection.

△ This cinderella, printed for the 1956 Olympic Games held in Australia, shows in its side borders the Olympic flame, which burned the whole time the games lasted.

△ Many countries print charity cinderellas as well as charity stamps. This pair of American cinderellas was sold to raise money for handicapped children. It was meant to be stuck on envelopes together with the postage stamps. The cinderella looks like a stamp but what is missing?

[Answer: A country name and value]

◁ This envelope was mailed in England on Christmas Eve in 1950. As well as a definitive stamp of King George VI, it carried an American Christmas greetings label. The U.S. prints special labels every Christmas. You can often find them in complete sheets for very low prices.

△ This is an environmental cinderella. It reminds people that pollution can damage the air we breathe and so damage our health. The butterflies shown on the cinderella represent the beauty of nature, which is also endangered by pollution. The Canada Trust, which printed it, helps protect the environment in Canada.

△ An international exhibition was held at Lyons, in France, in 1914: These were two stamplike labels issued to commemorate it. In the larger of the two, you can see the city of Lyons in the background. The exhibition, which was unfortunately interrupted by the start of World War I in August 1914, was intended to show the industry and agriculture of this area of France.

△ This bold cinderella label was issued for a two-day philatelic event held in 1916 at Palermo, on the Italian island of Sicily. The label shows a Red Cross. Can you find the Italian for "Red Cross" printed on it?

▷ Beer is an important product in Germany. This bright, jolly cinderella advertises a beer made by a Berlin brewery company. It shows a boy and girl in love—*Junge Liebe* means "young love"—enjoying a *stein*, or mug, of beer together.

◁ The British South Africa Company, which became Northern and Southern Rhodesia in 1924, issued this £100 stamp in 1901. It was not meant to be put on letters or even parcels, for £100 was enough to buy postage for ten thousand letters at the ordinary rate! This very high value was a "fiscal" and was used for revenue purposes. This meant it was used to pay duty or taxes on goods or services.

STAMP FINDER

The "philatelic" maps on the next four pages show the world as it is today. They show all the places that issue stamps and what is written on their stamps to tell you where they come from. Most country names listed in a catalog are easy to recognize from what is printed on their stamps. Where you see just a country name printed on the maps, you'll find the same name on its stamps. For example, Canada uses exactly the same name on its stamps as the English name of the country, so you will see just "Canada" on the map. Some countries have something slightly different on their stamps from the English name we have given it on the map. For example, Bahrain prints "State of Bahrain" on its stamps, and in cases like this you will just find "Bahrain" printed on the map. Many countries are republics, which can be printed as "République," "Republik," "Repoblik," "Republika" or "República," depending on the language. Republic is often shortened to "Rep" or just "R." In these cases we also print just the main part of the country's name, such as Malagasy instead of Republika Demokratika Malagasy, which is the full name printed on stamps from Malagasy. Other countries are much harder to recognize. For these we print the most usual words that appear on stamps in capital letters underneath the country's English name. So, for example, Albania has "RPS E SHQIPERISE" printed below it. Most countries that do not normally use the Latin alphabet also print their names in a Latin version. A few, however, do not, such as Russia. In these cases we print their names in their own alphabet under the English name.

But maps change from time to time (and they will go on changing long after this book is printed), and in the years since the first stamps they have changed a great deal. Some countries, once part of large empires, have become independent; others have become parts of bigger countries. Some countries have just changed their names. There are hundreds of these "philatelically terminated" countries, but you'll still find their stamps, so here is a list to help identify older stamps not shown on the map. We only have space to list the countries whose stamps you're most likely to find. The philatelically terminated name is listed in **CAPITAL LETTERS.** By the side of the name in capital letters is a brief description of the country, with the dates it issued stamps, printed like this: *1936–72*. The last date tells you when the last new stamp design was issued by the country. For example, the last new Gold Coast design was issued in 1954. Gold Coast became Ghana in 1957 and the first stamp with "Ghana" printed on it did not appear until 1957.

EUROPE

BADEN 1) Independent German duchy. *1851–68*. Now in West Germany. 2) Issues of French zone of occupied Germany *1947–49*. Now in West Germany.

BAYERN (Bavaria) Independent German state. *1849–1920*. Now in West Germany.

BÖHMEN UND MÄHREN (Bohemia and Moravia) Division of Czechoslovakia during German occupation *1939–45*. Rest of country became Slovakia (Slovensko). Returned to Czechoslovakia 1945.

DEUTSCHLAND (Germany) Military government of British and US zones of occupied Germany *1945–46*.

DEUTSCHE DEMOKRATISCHE REPUBLIK Used on East German stamps from 1950 till about 1968.

DEUTSCHE POST (German Post) Name on stamps of 1) British, US and Russian zones of occupied Germany *1946–49*. 2) West Germany *1949*. 3) West Berlin *1949–54*. 4) East Germany *1949*.

DEUTSCHES REICH (German Empire) Used on German stamps *1872–1945*.

LATVIJA (Latvia) Baltic state. *1918–40*. Now in Russia.

LIETUVA (Lithuania) Baltic state. *1918–40*. Now in Russia.

(Montenegro) *1874–1913/1941–44*. Now in Yugoslavia.

RHEINLAND-PFALZ (Rhineland Palatinate) French zone of occupied Germany *1947–49*.

SAAR/SAARLAND District of Germany *1920–35* and *1947–59*. Now in West Germany.

SACHSEN (Saxony) German state. *1850–63*. Now in West Germany.

СРБИЈА (Serbia) Independent kingdom. *1866–1918* and *1941–43*. Now in Yugoslavia.

SLOVENSKO (Slovakia) See Böhmen Und Mähren

SOWJETISCHE BEZATZUNGS ZONE (Soviet Russian Occupied Zone) Russian occupied zone in Germany. *1948*.

UKRAINE Independent state. *1918–23*. Now in Russia.

WÜRTTEMBERG 1) Independent German Kingdom. *1851–1920*. 2) Issues in part of French zone of occupied Germany. *1947–49*.

AFRICA

AFRIQUE EQUATORIALE FRANÇAISE (French Equatorial Africa) French colony made up of Gabon, Chad, Middle Congo, (see Moyen Congo) and Ubangi-Shari (now Central African Republic). *1935–58*. Colony broken up into independent states, all with own stamps.

AFRIQUE OCCIDENTALE FRANÇAISE (French West Africa) French colony made up of Senegal, French Guinea (now Guinea), Ivory Coast, Dahomey (now Benin), French Sudan (now Mali) Mauretania, Niger and Upper Volta (now Burkina Faso). *1944–59*. Colony now broken up into independent countries, all with own stamps.

BASUTOLAND British colony. *1933–66*. Now Lesotho.

BECHUANALAND British colony. *1885–1966*. Now Botswana.

BRITISH SOUTH AFRICA COMPANY See Rhodesia.
CAPE OF GOOD HOPE British colony. *1853–1904*. Now in South Africa.
CONGO BELGE/BELGISCH CONGO (Belgian Congo) Belgian colony 1909–60. See République Democratique du Congo.
GOLD COAST British colony. *1875–1954*. Now Ghana.
GUINÉ (Portuguese Guinea) Portuguese colony. *1881–1971*. Now Guinea-Bissau.
HAUTE VOLTA (Upper Volta) French colony. *1920–31* and *1959–84*. Independent 1960. Now Burkina Faso.
KENYA, UGANDA, TANGANYIKA Three British East African colonies that issued stamps as follows: East Africa and Uganda *1903–21*; Kenya and Uganda *1922–27*; Kenya, Uganda, Tanganyika *1935–64*; Kenya, Uganda, Tanzania *1965–76*. Tanganyika: German colony *1880–93*; used stamps of German East Africa *1893–1915*; British occupation *1915–22*; territory given to Britain by League of Nations *1922–27*; Tanganyika independent republic *1961–64*; joined by Zanzibar to form Tanzania 1964.
MAROC (Morocco) Stamp name of French Morocco *1914–56* and northern zone of independent Morocco – (1956–57). Now Royaume Du Maroc.
MOYEN CONGO (Middle Congo) French colony. Stamp name République du Congo. *1907–33*. See Afrique Equatoriale Française.
NORTHERN RHODESIA See Rhodesia.
NYASALAND British colony. Own stamps *1891–1950*. Now Malawi. See Rhodesia.
RHODESIA British colony in Africa, joined with Nyasaland 1954–64, issued stamps as follows: British South Africa Company *1892–1922*; divided into Northern Rhodesia, *1925–63*, and Southern Rhodesia, *1924–64*; joined again with Nyasaland to form Rhodesia and Nyasaland 1954–64; Rhodesia (former Southern Rhodesia, now Zimbabwe) *1965–78*.
RÉPUBLIQUE DEMOCRATIQUE DU CONGO (Congo Kinshasa) *1960–71*. Now Zaire.
RHODESIA AND NYASALAND see Rhodesia.
SOUTHERN RHODESIA See Rhodesia.
RUANDA URUNDI German colony occupied by Belgium. *1916–60*. Now separate states of Rwanda and Burundi.
SOMALIA Stamp name *1916–70*. Now J.D. Soomaliyeed.
SOMALILAND PROTECTORATE British protected territory. *1903–04*. Now in Somalia.
SOUTH AFRICA/SUID AFRIKA Country name on stamps in English and Afrikaans until 1966.
SOUTHWEST AFRICA/SUIDWES AFRIKA Country name on stamps in English, and Afrikaans until 1967. Now Namibia.
ZANZIBAR British colony. *1895–1965*.

THE MIDDLE EAST

ABU DHABI Trucial State, Persian Gulf. *1967–72*. Now in UAE (United Arab Emirates).
ADEN British colony. *1937–67*. Now in People's Democratic Republic of Yemen.
AJMAN As Abu Dhabi. *1964–72*.
FUJEIRA As Abu Dhabi. *1964–72*.
IRAN Stamp name for Iran *1936–38* and *1948–79*. Now Islamic Republic of Iran. (R.I. Iran or I.R. Iran)
LIBAN Stamp name for Lebanon. See République Libanaise.
PALESTINE Ottoman Turkish colony. Under British rule 1923–1948. Stamps issued for various parts of this area after 1948 by Israel (1948 onwards), Jordan

(*1948–50*) and Egypt (Gaza) *1948–67*.
POSTE PERSANE (Persian Post) Stamp name for Persia (now Iran) *1868–1935*.
RAS AL KHAIMA Sheikdom on Persian Gulf. *1964–72*. Now in UAE.
RÉPUBLIQUE LIBANAISE (Lebanese Republic) Stamp name for Lebanon.
SHARJAH As Abu Dhabi. *1963–68*.
MANAMA Dependency of Ajman. Now in UAE. *1966–72*.
UAE (United Arab Emirates) Union of Abu Dhabi, Ajman, Dubai, Fujeira, Ras Al Khaima, Sharjah and Umm Al Qiwain. First UAE stamp issued 1973.
UMM AL QIWAIN As Abu Dhabi. *1964–67*.

ASIA

CAMBODGE (Cambodia) Part of French colony of Indochina. *1951–71*. Now Kampuchea.
CEYLON British colony. *1857–1972*. Independent 1948. Now Sri Lanka.
ÉTABLISSEMENTS FRANÇAIS DANS L'INDE (French Indian Settlements) French colony. *1892–1954*. Joined India 1954.
INDOCHINE (Indochina) French colony made up of Vietnam (independent 1954) Laos (independent 1951) and Cambodia (independent 1954). *1889–1949*.
JAPAN Stamps marked ● *1872–1947*; 日 本 郵 便 *1947–1966*. Stamp name now NIPPON.
ROYAUME DU LAOS (Kingdom of Laos) Part of French colony of Indochina. *1951–75*. Stamp name now Postes Lao.
STRAITS SETTLEMENTS British colony. *1867–1941*. Now Malaysia.
NORTH BORNEO British colony. *1883–1963*. Now state of Sabah in Malaysia.
SARAWAK British protectorate and colony. *1869–1963*. Now in Malaysia.
SIAM *1883–1939*. Now Thailand.

THE AMERICAS

ANTIOQUIA One of seven states of Granadine Confederation. *1868–1903*. Now part of Colombia.
BRITISH GUIANA British colony. *1850–1966*. Now Guyana.
BRITISH HONDURAS British colony. *1858–1973*. Now Belize.
GUYANE FRANÇAISE (French Guiana) French colony. *1886–1947*. Now uses French stamps.
NEWFOUNDLAND State of Canada. *1857–1947*. Now part of Canada.

AUSTRALIA

The following territories were separate Australian states. All now use Australian stamps, but issued their own as shown.
NEW SOUTH WALES *1850–1912*: **QUEENSLAND** *1860–1912*: **VICTORIA** *1850–1912*: **WESTERN AUSTRALIA** *1854–1912*.

PACIFIC OCEAN

ÉTABLISSEMENTS FRANÇAIS DE L'OCÉANIE (French Oceanic Settlements) French colony. *1892–1956*. Now French Polynesia.
WESTERN SAMOA *1914–55*. Now Samoa I Sisifo.

THE CARIBBEAN

LEEWARD ISLANDS British colony. *1890–1953*. Made up of Antigua, Barbuda, Virgin Islands, Dominica, Montserrat, Nevis, St Christopher (St Kitts). Now separated each with own stamps.
MARTINIQUE French colony. *1886–1947*. Now uses French stamps.
ST CHRISTOPHER-NEVIS-ANGUILLA Stamp name of St Kitts-Nevis (British colony) from *1952–80*. St Kitts and Nevis issued stamps separately from 1980. See Leeward Islands.

STAMP MAPS

North and South America/Europe

Greenland
GRØNLAND

Canada

Saint Pierre and Miquelon
SAINT-PIERRE ET MIQUELON

United States
USA

New York (UN)

Bermuda

NORTH ATLANTIC OCEAN

PACIFIC OCEAN

Cuba

Dominican Republic
REPUBLICA DOMINICANA

Mexico

Cayes
of Belize

Haiti

Caribbean Islands

Belize

Guatemala Honduras

Netherlands Antilles
NEDERLANDSE ANTILLEN

Grenadines of Saint Vincent

El Salvador Nicaragua

Grenadines of Grenada

Costa Rica

Bahamas

Panama

Venezuela Guyana Surinam
SURINAME

Turks and
Caicos Islands

Anguilla

Saint Kitts

Colombia

French
Guiana
Uses French
Stamps

British
Virgin
Islands

Nevis

Barbuda
Antigua

Ecuador

Cayman
Islands

Redonda
Montserrat

Dominica

Jamaica

Caicos
Islands

Saint Vincent
Bequia

Saint Lucia

Peru

Brazil
BRASIL

Aruba

Union Island
Grenada

Barbados

Trinidad
and Tobago

Bolivia

Pacific Islands

Tuvalu

Paraguay

Wallis
and Futuna
WALLIS ET FUTUNA

Tokelau

Penrhyn

Chile

Fiji

Samoa
SAMOA I SISIFO

Niuafo'ou

Niue

French Polynesia
POLYNESIE
FRANCAISE RF

Pitcairn
Islands

Argentina

Tonga

Uruguay

Cook
Islands

SOUTH ATLANTIC OCEAN

Islands of Tuvalu
Funafati
Nanumaga
Nanumea
Niutao
Nui
Nukefetau
Nukulaelae
Vaitupu

Falkland Islands

South Georgia and the
South Sandwich Islands

United Nations stamps are issued by its three
headquarters, New York (USA), Geneva
(Switzerland) and Vienna (Austria). Their stamps
are marked with one or more of the following, all of
which mean United Nations in different languages:
UNITED NATIONS
NATIONS UNIES
NACIONES UNIDAS
VEREINTE NATIONEN
VEREINTEN NATIONEN
ОБЪЕДИНЕННЫЕ НАЦИИ
联合国

**NORTH
ATLANTIC
OCEAN**

Iceland
ÍSLAND

Faroe Islands
FØRAYAR

Finland

Norway
NORGE/NOREG

Sweden
SVERIGE

Scotland

Åland
Islands

Russia
ПОУTA CCCP

Northern
Ireland

Isle of Man

Denmark
DANMARK

East Germany
DDR/DEUTSCHE DEMOKRATISCHE REPUBLIK

West Berlin
DEUTSCHE BUNDESPOST BERLIN

Ireland
EIRE

Great
Britain

Wales

Netherlands
NEDERLAND

Poland
POLSKA

Czechoslovakia
ČESKOSLOVENSKO

Alderney
Guernsey
Jersey

Belgium
BELGIQUE-BELGIE

West
Germany
DEUTSCHE
BUNDESPOST

Hungary
MAGYAR POSTA

France
RÉPUBLIQUE FRANÇAISE

Luxembourg

Austria
REPUBLIK
ÖSTERREICH

Vienna (UN)

France also issues stamps
for the Council of Europe
(CONSEIL DE L'EUROPE)
and UNESCO

Geneva
(UN)

Rumania
POSTA ROMANA

Liechtenstein

Portugal

Monaco
Switzerland
HELVETIA

Yugoslavia
JUGOSLAVIJA

Bulgaria
БЪЛГАРИЯ

Spain
ESPAÑA

French Andorra
('POSTES' = French)

San Marino

Italy
ITALIA

Turkey
TÜRKIYE CUMHURIYETI

Gibraltar

Spanish Andorra
('CORREOS' = Spanish)

Vatican City
POSTE VATICANE/
POSTA VATICANA

Greece
ΕΛΛΑΣ
ΕΛΛΗΝΙΚΗ
ΔΗΜΟΚΡΑΤΙΑ

Cyprus (Turkish)
KUZEY KIBRIS TURK
CUMHURIYETI

Syria

Iraq

Albania
RPS E SHQIPERISE

Malta

Lebanon
LIBAN

Cyprus (Greek)

Israel

Jordan

MEDITERRANEAN SEA

STAMP MAPS

Africa, Australasia, Asia

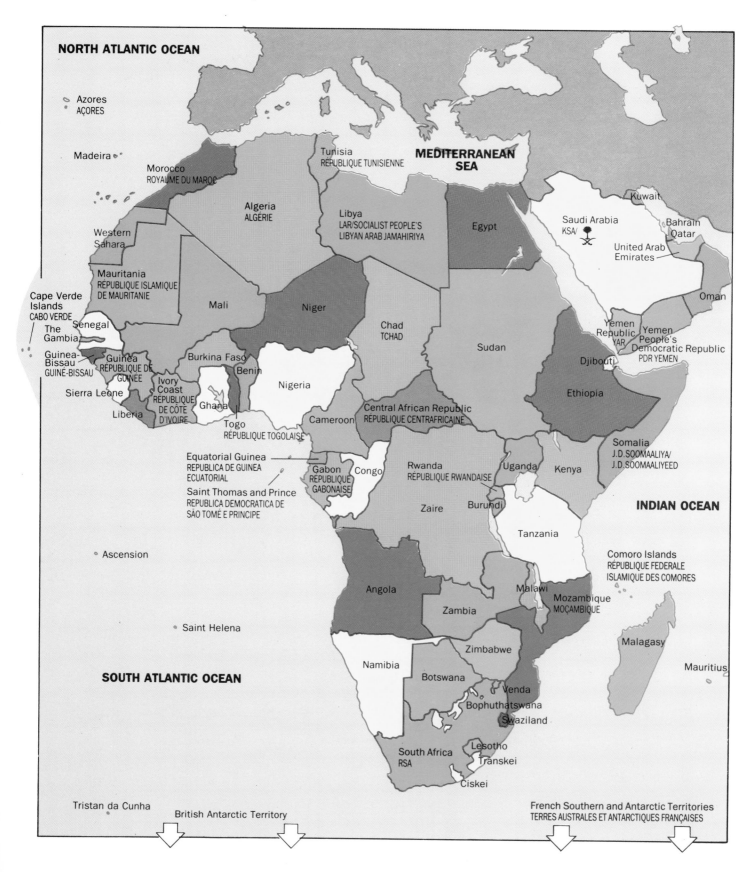

NORTH ATLANTIC OCEAN

Azores
AÇORES

Madeira

Morocco
ROYAUME DU MAROC

Tunisia
RÉPUBLIQUE TUNISIENNE

MEDITERRANEAN
SEA

Kuwait

Algeria
ALGÉRIE

Libya
LAR/SOCIALIST PEOPLE'S
LIBYAN ARAB JAMAHIRIYA

Egypt

Saudi Arabia
KSA/

Bahrain
Qatar

Western
Sahara

United Arab
Emirates

Mauritania
RÉPUBLIQUE ISLAMIQUE
DE MAURITANIE

Oman

Cape Verde
Islands
CABO VERDE

Mali

Niger

Chad
TCHAD

Sudan

Yemen
Republic
YAR

Yemen
People's
Democratic Republic
PDR YEMEN

The
Gambia

Senegal

Guinea-
Bissau
GUINÉ-BISSAU

Guinea
RÉPUBLIQUE DE
GUINÉE

Burkina Faso

Benin

Djibouti

Sierra Leone

Ivory
Coast
RÉPUBLIQUE
DE CÔTE
D'IVOIRE

Ghana

Nigeria

Ethiopia

Liberia

Togo
RÉPUBLIQUE TOGOLAISE

Cameroon

Central African Republic
RÉPUBLIQUE CENTRAFRICAINE

Somalia
J.D.SOOMAALIYA/
J.D.SOOMAALIYEED

Equatorial Guinea
REPUBLICA DE GUINEA
ECUATORIAL

Gabon
RÉPUBLIQUE
GABONAISE

Congo

Rwanda
RÉPUBLIQUE RWANDAISE

Uganda

Kenya

INDIAN OCEAN

Saint Thomas and Prince
REPUBLICA DEMOCRATICA DE
SÃO TOMÉ E PRINCIPE

Zaire

Burundi

Ascension

Tanzania

Comoro Islands
RÉPUBLIQUE FEDERALE
ISLAMIQUE DES COMORES

Angola

Malawi

Mozambique
MOÇAMBIQUE

Saint Helena

Zambia

Malagasy

Zimbabwe

Mauritius

SOUTH ATLANTIC OCEAN

Namibia

Botswana

Venda
Bophuthatswana
Swaziland

South Africa
RSA

Lesotho
Transkei

Ciskei

Tristan da Cunha

British Antarctic Territory

French Southern and Antarctic Territories
TERRES AUSTRALES ET ANTARCTIQUES FRANÇAISES

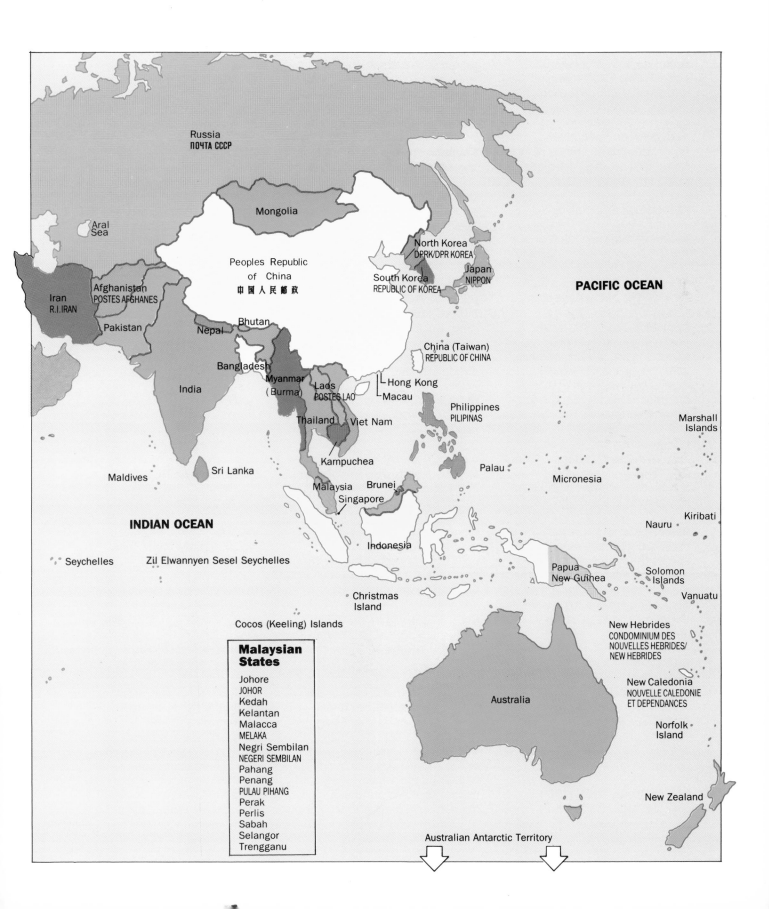

Russia
ПОЧТА СССР

Mongolia

Aral
Sea

Peoples Republic
of China
中国人民邮政

North Korea
DPRK/DPR KOREA

Japan
NIPPON

South Korea
REPUBLIC OF KOREA

PACIFIC OCEAN

Iran
R.I.IRAN

Afghanistan
POSTES AFGHANES

Pakistan

Bhutan

Nepal

Bangladesh

India

Myanmar
(Burma)

Laos
POSTES LAO

China (Taiwan)
REPUBLIC OF CHINA

Hong Kong

Macau

Thailand

Viet Nam

Philippines
PILIPINAS

Marshall
Islands

Kampuchea

Palau

Micronesia

Maldives

Sri Lanka

Malaysia

Brunei

Singapore

Nauru

Kiribati

INDIAN OCEAN

Indonesia

Seychelles

Zil Elwannyen Sesel Seychelles

Papua
New Guinea

Solomon
Islands

Vanuatu

Christmas
Island

Cocos (Keeling) Islands

New Hebrides
CONDOMINIUM DES
NOUVELLES HEBRIDES/
NEW HEBRIDES

**Malaysian
States**

Johore
JOHOR
Kedah
Kelantan
Malacca
MELAKA
Negri Sembilan
NEGERI SEMBILAN
Pahang
Penang
PULAU PIHANG
Perak
Perlis
Sabah
Selangor
Trengganu

Australia

New Caledonia
NOUVELLE CALEDONIE
ET DEPENDANCES

Norfolk
Island

New Zealand

Australian Antarctic Territory

GLOSSARY 1

Adhesive A postage stamp issued after 1840 that has adhesive (gum) on its back for sticking it onto envelopes.

Aerogramme Special letter made for sending by air. Made of light paper that can be folded and sealed by gummed tabs.

Airmail Sending mail by air.

Aniline A "fugitive" ink that will run if soaked in water. Used to stop people from using stamps twice. Aniline ink shows its color through the back of the stamp.

Approvals Stamps in small books or on cards sent by dealers in the mail. These are sent "on approval," which means collectors choose the stamps they want to buy and return the rest with their payment.

Bilingual Stamps inscribed or printed in two languages. French and Flemish, for example, are used on stamps of Belgium, where both are spoken.

Bisect A stamp cut in half, usually diagonally (on a slant) across the stamp. Used on an envelope, a bisect has half the value of the complete stamp. Bisects have been used where there is a shortage of low value stamps.

Block More than four stamps joined together in a square or oblong shape.

Bogus A pretend stamp, for instance from a country that does not exist. Made to cheat collectors.

Booklet Pane Small stiff-covered book of stamps in panes (like a **Block**) sewn together on the left-hand side. Stamp panes may alternate with other panes showing post office and other advertisements.

Cachet A special instruction or message printed on an envelope.

Cancel/Cancellation Postmark on a stamp, which shows it has been used for postage.

Canceled To Order See **CTO**.

Chalk-Surfaced A chalky coating put onto stamp paper. The stamps look shiny because, in time, the chalk "polishes" the surface. Chalk-surfaced stamps also have watermarks that are difficult to see.

Classic Early stamps issued up to about 1900, which are either rare or beautifully designed and printed.

Coil A stamp from a roll of stamps dispensed by automatic stamp vending (selling) machines.

Color Trial Test of a stamp design, printed in different colors to find out which are the best to use. Color trials are types of proofs.

Comb Perforation Created by a perforating machine that has perforating pins arranged like a comb.

Commemorative Stamp or set for events like anniversaries and other special occasions.

Controls Letters and numbers printed in the margins of sheets of stamps to make it easier for the printer to check that the stamps have been correctly printed.

Corner Block Block of stamps (See **Block**) taken from the top or bottom corners of a sheet of stamps. The sheet margin is still attached to the block.

Counterfeit See **Forgery**.

Cover Collectors' name for an envelope.

CTO Short for "canceled to order," meaning stamps that are specially canceled for collectors, with very neat, clean postmarks. Often, they are not sent through the post in the ordinary way or even stuck onto envelopes. CTO stamps may still have gum on the back.

CWO Cash with order, that is, sending payment for stamps when you order them.

Cylinder Number Number printed in the margins of sheets of stamps to show which printing cylinder has been used.

Definitive Ordinary stamps issued for regular use on mail.

Denomination The value printed on a stamp, or what it would cost you to buy it in a post office.

Die The original engraved proofing plate made for a recess-printed stamp design.

Doctor Blade A special steel blade used to wipe ink from a gravure stamp printing cylinder.

Embossing Producing a stamp by pressing the design onto paper.

Entire An envelope with the original letter still inside.

Error A mistake in the design or printing of a stamp, usually a very obvious one, such as an inverted center. See also **Flaw** or **Variety**, words that are sometimes used to describe an error.

Essay Trial design for a stamp. When new stamps are planned, several designers are asked to send in essays, but only one of them gets the job. The other designs remain as essays only.

Facsimile An exact copy of a stamp.

Face Value The value printed on the "face" or front of a stamp. See **Denomination**.

Fake A real stamp or postmark altered to cheat collectors. A low denomination stamp may be altered to a higher denomination, which is more expensive.

Fault Damage on a stamp, such as missing perforations, tears, stains or thinning of the paper, which happens when a layer of paper is torn off.

FDC See **First Day Cover**.

FDI See **First Day of Issue**.

Fine Used See **FU**.

First Day Cover A cover with stamps postmarked and sent through the mail on the first day they were sold in a post office. Special covers and postmarks are usually used for this.

First Day of Issue The first day a stamp is officially sold to the public.

Fiscal A stamp used to show that tax or duty has been paid. Fiscals are not usually used for postage.

Flaw An error, usually small, that occurs when a stamp is being printed.

Forgery A counterfeit or illegal copy of a real stamp or postmark.

Frank Another word for postmark.

FU Fine used, that is, with a light, neat cancellation.

Fugitive Ink See **Aniline**.

Gravure See **Stamp Printing: Photogravure**.

Gutter A strip of paper between rows of stamps on a sheet. Usually plain but sometimes with "traffic lights," that is, circles of the different colors used to print the stamp.

Hand Stamp Postmark put on an envelope by hand rather than by machine.

Heavy Hinge See **HH**.

HH Heavy hinge. A hinge on a mounted mint stamp that cannot be removed from the back of the stamp without damaging it.

Imperf Imperforate or without perforations.

Imperforate See **Imperf**.

Intaglio See **Stamp Printing: Recess**.

Inscription Words printed on a stamp design describing what the stamp shows or why it has been issued.

Inverted Upside-down. Used to describe watermarks, centers or frames on stamps.

Killer A canceler that puts a very heavy postmark on a stamp to hide the design completely. This is to prevent the postmark from being washed off the stamp so that the stamp can be reused. Also called an obliterator.

Kiloware Stamps on paper (cut-off envelopes or card) that are sold by weight.

Laid Paper Paper that has a lined texture to it.

Line Engraved Lines engraved

on steel or copper plates. Used in recess printing. See **Stamp Printing: Recess Printing**.

Lithography See **Stamp Printing: Lithography**.

Local Stamp for use in a particular area rather than all over a country.

Lozenge Cancellation filled with bars in an oval shape.

LHM Lightly hinged mint. This means that the hinge on a mint stamp has made only a small mark on the gum at the back of the stamp.

Lightly Hinged Mint See **LHM**.

Margins The plain space between a stamp design and the perforations or, in an imperforate stamp, the plain paper around the edge of the design.

Meter Mark Stamp and postmark printed all-in-one on a letter by a special machine.

Miniature Sheet Sheet with stamp or stamps perforated into it or with stamp designs printed on it. Similar to a souvenir sheet.

MM Mounted mint, that is, an unused stamp with gum on the back that has been hinged. See also **LHM** and **HH**.

Mounted Mint See **MM**.

Mulready British pictorial envelopes and letter sheets of 1840 printed by William Mulready, a stationery designer.

Multiple More than one stamp joined together by their margins. See **Block** and **Sheet**.

Obliterator See **Killer**

Official Stamp overprinted with

GLOSSARY 2

"Official" or "Service," for use by government departments.

Offset Lithography See **Stamp Printing: Offset Lithography**.

Overprint Words or numbers printed onto an existing stamp to mark an event, increase the stamp's value (See **Surcharge**) or authorize it for use in another country; for example, Gibraltar's first stamps were issues of Bermuda, overprinted "Gibraltar."

Omnibus Large series of stamps or sets issued by different countries at the same time to mark the same event.

OG Original gum, that is, the gum put on a stamp when it was first made. Used when describing early stamps to show that they have not been regummed. See **Regummed**.

Original Gum See **OG**.

Pane See **Booklet Pane**.

Perfin Initials, usually of a business company, perforated into stamps for use on mail sent by that company.

Perforation The jagged edges around a stamp made when it is separated from a sheet that has holes between each row of stamps.

Phosphor Usually refers to a stamp coated with phosphorus, a glowing substance, either in lines or with all-over coating. These lines are usually hard to see with the naked eye but special post office machines can detect them and so speed up sorting the mail.

Photogravure See **Stamp Printing: Photogravure**.

Plate Number Number printed in the margin or other part of a stamp design to show which plate was used in printing. Mostly refers to earlier stamps issued before 1900.

Pochette Transparent plastic envelope or "pocket" often used for displaying stamps.

Postage Due Special stamp put on a letter that does not have enough postage on it. The receiver of the letter pays the extra amount.

Postal History Collectors' term for covers and the information given by their cancellations, cachets and other marks.

Postal Stationery Specially made envelopes or letter forms for use in the mail. See **Aerogrammes** and **PSE**.

Pre-Adhesive Mail sent before adhesive (gummed) prepaid postage began in 1840. See also **Pre-Stamp.**

Pre-Cancel Stamps with a semi-circular "cancel" printed in the design. Letters carrying pre-cancels do not have to be postmarked, thus helping to speed up the mails.

Postmark see **Cancel Cancellation**.

Presentation Pack A mint set of stamps in a special folder that also has information about the stamps and why they were issued.

Pre-Stamp Mail before 1840. See **Pre-Adhesive**.

Pre-Stamped Envelope See **PSE**.

Priced To Sell At See **PTSA**.

Proof A test printing of a stamp from an original plate or die.

Provisionals Emergency stamps issued to be used for a short time only, for example, when a country occupies another country during a war.

PSE Pre-stamped envelope, that is, an envelope with a stamp printed onto it.

PTSA Priced to sell at. Usually describes circuit club books and other items that have been put into auctions with their original prices still on them.

Recess See **Stamp Printing: Recess**.

Reentry Parts of plates for engraved stamps often get damaged or worn. To save making a whole new plate, these areas may be corrected by hand and reengraved. Sometimes part of the old damaged plate is left in, though not in exactly the same position as the new correction. If this happens, both old and new parts will print and the stamp will appear to have been printed twice in this area.

Regionals Stamps printed for use in regions or parts of a country, such as Scotland or Wales, parts of Great Britain.

Regummed Older mint stamps may lose their gum (See **OG/ Original Gum**) but have had new gum put on the back to cheat collectors.

Reprint Stamps printed from the original plates after the stamps are no longer sold in post offices.

Retouch Small correction made

by hand on a plate or cylinder for printing engraved stamps. See **Reentry**.

Rouletted Cuts made between stamps on a sheet that enable them to be separated. Another form of perforation.

Revenue Stamp See **Fiscal**.

Se-Tenant Stamps of different design attached to each other by their perforations.

Shade A slightly different red, blue, green or other hue of a stamp color.

Souvenir Sheet Similar to **Miniature Sheet**.

Spacefiller An imperfect or damaged stamp that fills a gap in a collection and that would usually be expensive. The collector may not be able to afford a better copy.

Specimen An example of a stamp, with "Specimen" overprinted onto or perforated into it in order to stop people from using them in the mail.

Sheet A complete sheet of stamps with margins all around as supplied to the post office. When you buy stamps there, these are taken from the sheets.

Stamp Printing
  Letterpress Method of printing from a printing surface that is raised above the rest of the non-printing plate. Often called **Typography** or **Surface Printing**.
  Lithography Surface printing using a flat plate.
  Offset Lithography A more modern version of lithography. Instead of printing directly from the plate, as in ordinary lithography, the ink on the plate is first transferred to another roller. It is from this roller that the paper picks up the ink and is printed.
  Photogravure A type of recess printing, using plates etched by photography. Also called gravure for short.
  Recess Printing Printing stamps by forcing ink into recesses, or spaces engraved below the surface of a printing plate. Also called **Intaglio**.

Strip Three or more of the same stamps joined together horizontally (side by side) or vertically (one below the other).

Surcharge An extra value overprinted onto a stamp.

Surface-Printed See **Stamp Printing: Letterpress**.

Sweat Box Plastic box with lid containing a sponge moistened with cold water. For removing old hinges from stamps or getting stamps off paper. Place stamps on wet sponge. Close the lid and leave for at least thirty minutes.

Tab An extra piece of paper perforated to the bottom of a stamp.

Tête Bêche A pair of joined stamps with one the right way up and the other upside down.

Tied A stamp is "tied" to a cover when the postmark is placed over the edge of the stamp and onto the enevelope.

Traffic Lights See **Gutter**.

Typography See **Stamp Printing: Letterpress**.

UM Unmounted mint, or a stamp that has never been hinged.

Unchecked A collection or packet containing stamps that may have varieties, like inverted watermarks. The seller has not checked the stamps to see exactly what they are, so the buyer could find bargains there.

Underprint Words or symbols printed onto the back of a stamp, under the gum.

Ungummed Without gum. Often used to describe a stamp with no postmark but with no gum, either. It may have been used, but the postmark missed it, or it may be mint and the gum has been washed off.

Unissued Stamps printed for use but never issued because, for instance, the government that ordered them has been overthrown in a revolution.

Unmounted Mint See **UM**.

Used Abroad Stamps with postmarks from outside the country that issued them. Often used by armies or expeditions that take their own country's stamps overseas for use on letters home. Stamps used abroad can be identified by their foreign postmarks.

Variety See **Error**.

Very Fine Used See **VFU**.

VFU Very fine used, that is, with a very light postmark.

Vignette Center picture that gradually shades off to plain paper in a stamp design.

Watermark A symbol in stamp paper, which can be seen where the paper is slightly thinner.

Wing Margin An extra-wide margin on one side of a stamp.

Wove Paper Paper with a smooth, even texture.

PARTS OF A STAMP

Some stamps carry an enormous amount of information about themselves. You can see this from the labels pointing to the different parts of this French stamp, which has been greatly enlarged. Not all stamps will give you this amount of information but some give even more and may include the stamp printer's name.

Logo: A special sign or symbol used by an organization. This stamp was issued to tell people about the work of UNESCO, an international organization that is concerned with education and health welfare, so their logo is printed on the stamp. The Red Cross is another logo.

Postal use: This tells you what sort of mail the stamp is used for. This stamp was for ordinary mails. Other uses might be airmail or postage due.

Value: The cost of the stamp in a post office, in this case, 1 franc 70 centimes or just 1,70. Many countries do not print the actual currency on the stamp.

Perforation: The rows of holes punched through the edges of a stamp so you can easily remove it from a sheet without damaging it. These are sometimes called "teeth." The size and number of perforations varies from stamp to stamp.

Gum: This is on the back of the stamp and sticks a stamp to a letter.

Margin: The plain space between the perforations and the stamp design.

Subject of the stamp: This stamp was issued for the International Year of the Child. Other stamps could tell you what they commemorate, or the name of a ship illustrated.

Designer: Odette Baillais, the artist who designed the stamp.

Engraver: P. Forget engraved the stamp onto a block of metal.

Year of issue: 1979 was when the stamp was first issued. Not all countries show this but it is becoming more common.

Country of issue: Today, every country but one prints its name on its stamps; Great Britain is the only one that does not.

FINDING OUT MORE

NATIONAL ORGANIZATIONS
American Philatelic Society
P.O. Box 8000
State College, PA 16803

Junior Philatelists of America
Central Office
P.O. Box 15329
San Antonio, TX 78212

Philatelic Foundation
21 E. 40th Street
New York, NY 10016

CLUBS
The U.S. Postal Service sponsors 35,000 Benjamin Franklin Stamp Clubs (BFSCs) in public and private elementary schools throughout the nation. BFSC members receive an edition of the *Treasury of Stamps* album, an *Introduction to Stamp Collecting* booklet, bimonthly newsletters, and have access to films (available on a loan basis from the Postal Service). If you are interested in starting a BFSC in your school, have one of your teachers or administrators contact your local postmaster or write to: U.S. Postal Service, Ben Franklin Stamp Club Program, Washington, DC 20260.

If you are a junior high or high school student and are looking for a local club to join, write to Linn's Club Center, P.O. Box 29, Sidney, OH 45365. They will send you information on clubs located in your zip code area.

CATALOGS
Scott Standard Postage Stamp Catalogue. Issued annually by Scott Publishing Company, Sidney, Ohio. Four volumes providing current values and descriptions for all postage stamps ever issued in the world.

Scott United States Stamp Catalogue. Issued annually by Scott Publishing Company, Sidney, Ohio. Comprehensive price catalog for all United States Stamps and their varieties.

The Postal Guide to U.S. Stamps. A 300-page illustrated reference guide for young stamp collectors, available in most school libraries or post offices throughout the country.

MAGAZINES/NEWSPAPERS
Linn's Stamp News, P.O. Box 29, Sidney, OH 45365. The largest weekly stamp newspaper.

Stamp Collector, Box 10, Albany, OR 97321. Weekly for beginning and advanced collectors.

Stamps Magazine, 85 Canisteo Street, Hornell, NY 14843. The weekly magazine of philately.

FREE MATERIALS
Stamp Collecting Made Easy, P.O. Box 29, Sidney, OH 45365. A free, illustrated 96-page booklet.

Introduction to Stamp Collecting and *The Wonderful World of Stamps*, both available by writing to: United States Postal Service, Philatelic Sales Division, P.O. Box 449998, Kansas City, MO 64144.

INDEX

This index is meant to be used together with Stamp Finder (pages 82–83) and the Glossary (pages 88–91). Between them, these three sections should give you most of the subjects you will need to look up. Thematic subjects are listed in alphabetical order under "Thematics" in the index. We have listed only the most popular thematic subjects here. **Bold** numbers in the index refer to pictures or subjects mentioned in the captions to the pictures.

Afghanistan **6**
Aircraft:
   see Thematics: Aircraft
Airmail **14**, **29**, **34**, 44, **57**, **58**, **59**, 59, 88
Albums 12, **13**, 40, **68**, **69**, 69, 71
America, North **20**, 20, 59
America, South **8**, 17, 20, 59, 62
American Civil War **32**
American Revolution 63
Animals: see Thematics: Animals
Approvals, stamp 50, 88
Arctic Circle **25**
Auctions, stamp **29**, 49, 53
Australia **11**, 19, 33, **46**, **54**, **56**, **79**, 80, 83
Austria **3**, **4**, **9**, 30, **34**, 35, 39, 47, **54**, 60, **63**, **77**
Automobiles:
   see Thematics: Automobiles

Balloons **48**, **58**, **59**, 59
Belgium **12**, 14, **34**, 35, **41**, **54**, **73**, **76**, 83, 88
Benjamin and Sarpy (forgers) **46**, 47:
   see also: Forgery
Bhutan **42**, **43**, 43
Bicycles: see Thematics: Bicycles
Booklet 40, **41**, 73
Booklet pane **40**, 88

Boston Tea Party (American Revolution) 63
Bottle Post **9**, 60
Boy Scouts: see Thematics: Boy Scouts
Brazil 17, **24**, 35, **57**, 57, **58**
Britain **5**, **7**, **9**, **10**, 10, **12**, **14**, **19**, **22**, **23**, 23, **28**, **33**, **34**, 35, **39**, **40**, 40, **41**, **44**, **45**, **46**, **55**, **56**, **57**, **58**, 59, 60, **62**, **63**, 64, **65**, **72**, **73**, **75**, **76**, **77**, **78**, 79, **80**, 82, 83, 92, **93**, 93
British Commonwealth: see Commonwealth, British
British Guiana 29, **56**, 57, 83
Butterflies: see Thematics: Butterflies

Canada 17, 17, 20, **32**, 33, **41**, **54**, **59**, **81**, 82, 83
Cape of Good Hope (Africa) 43, **57**, 57, 83
Catalogs **12**, 12, **13**, 14, 20, 30, 33, 49, **52**, **54**, 54, **55**, 67, 71, 80
Ceylon 33, 83:
   see also Sri Lanka
China 6, 8, **30**, 30, 33, **54**
Cinderella stamps 63, **80**, 80, **81**
Clubs, stamp 14, **52**, 53, 93
Collectors, famous **28**, **29**, 29:
   see also Ferrary, Philippe von
Collectors, royal **28**:
   see also George V, George VI (kings of England)
Commemorative stamps **14**, **33**, 35, 54, 57, 88; apart from those listed, most stamps with special pictures that are illustrated in the book are commemoratives.
Commonwealth, British **28**, **54**, **55**, **72**
Concorde (aircraft) **18**

Covers **22**, 27, **44**, 44, **45**, 88: see also Postal history
Definitive stamps **10**, 10, **14**, 35, **75**, 88
Denmark **54**, **55**, 59, **64**, **67**, **76**
Dinosaurs: see Thematics: Dinosaurs
Disney, Walt **16**
Dominica 17, 83
Dutch stamps: see Netherlands

East Germany **14**, **31**, 74, 82: see also Germany
Egypt 8, **28**, 60, 83
Embossed stamps **39**, 88
Engraved stamps 17, **37**, **38**, **39**, **55**, 76, 77, 89, 90, 91, **92**
Errors 7, **41**, **54**, 54, **57**, **74**, 74, 75, 88: see also Varieties
Europa stamps **39**, **52**, **72**, 73, **76**
Exhibitions, stamp 14, 24, 40, **52**, **53**, 53, **56**, 79, 80, **81**
Express stamps **35**, 35

Fairs, stamp 14, **49**, 49, 50
Faroe Islands **54**
FDC: see First Day Cover
Ferrary, Phillipe von 27, **28**, **29**, 29
Finland **9**, **11**, **19**, **74**
First Day Covers 44, **45**, **48**, **54**, **68**, 73, 89
Fiscals 80, **81**, 89:
   see also Cinderella stamps
Flaw 89: see also Error; Varieties
Flowers: see Thematics: Flowers
Forgery **10**, **46**, **47**, 47, 64, **65**, 89: see also Benjamin and Sarpy; Fournier, François; Sperati, Juan de
Fournier, François 47:
   see also Forgery
France **8**, **10**, **12**, **14**, **18**, **20**, **25**, **26**, 27, **31**, **33**,

34, **35**, **38**, 39, 40, **41**, **45**, 47, **49**, **54**, **57**, **58**, **60**, 60, 61, 62, **63**, 64, **65**, **72**, **76**, 76, **77**, **78**, **79**, **81**, 82, 83, 88, **92**, 92
Franklin, Benjamin 10
Fugitive ink 51, 88, 89

George V, King of England **28**, **29**
George VI, King of England **28**, **29**, **65**, **75**, **80**
Germany **5**, 8, **9**, **11**, **13**, **14**, **16**, **18**, 27, **31**, 33, **37**, **39**, **40**, 40, **46**, **54**, **58**, 60, **61**, **62**, 62, **63**, **64**, **65**, 73, 74, **81**, 82
Ghana 33, 33, 82, 83
Gibbons, Stanley **54**, **55** 93
Giroux, Hector: see Stamp murder
Gold Coast 33, 33, 82, 83
Gravure: see Photogravure
Great Britain: see Britain
Greece **30**
Gum 23, 67, 69, 80, 88, 89, 90, 91, 92

Hawaii **19**, 27, 33, **57**
Hill, Rowland **10**, 10
Hinges, stamp **68**, **69**, 89
Hitler, Adolf **46**, **65**
Hong Kong **6**
Hungary **16**, 30, **67**, **73**

Imperforate Stamps 23, **41**, **75**, 89
India **6**, **45**, 59
Intaglio 39, 89: see also Engraved stamps and Recess printing
Ireland 65
Italy **7**, **8**, **11**, **18**, 24, **25**, 33, **34**, **35**, **43**, **56**, **59**, 59, 60, **61**, **64**, **65**, **78**, **81**

Japan **19**, 30, **31**, 40, 57, **79**, 79, 83

Kiloware 50, **51**, 89

Laos **31**, **70**, 83
Latvia 43, 82
Leroux, Gaston: see Stamp murder

Letter carrier **8**, **9**, 10
Letterpress **38**, 38, 90, 91
Lithography **38**, 39, 89, 91

"Machin" stamps 35
Magazines, stamp 14, 93
Mail coaches **9**
Mailman **8**, 8, **9**, **61**
Maltese Cross cancellation **23**, 79
"Marianne" stamps **14**, 35, **55**
Maximum Cards 40, **41**
Mexico 24, **47**, **58**, 62
Miniature sheets **40**, 40, **54**, 73, 89: see also Souvenir sheets
Moens, J.B. **12**
Music: see Thematics: Music

Netherlands **7**, **11**, **16**, 24, **38**, **39**, **47**, **49**, **54**, **55**, **61**, **64**, **65**, **68**, **73**
New South Wales (Australia) **46**, 83
New Zealand **17**, 19, 64
Norway **9**, **19**, **62**

Official stamps 35, 80, **81**, 89, 90
Offset lithography: see Lithography
Olympic Games **22**, **73**, 73, 80

Pakistan **6**
Panama Canal **27**, **78**
Pane: see Booklet pane
Paquebot (ship mail) 44
Parcel Post **35**, 35
Paris (France) **25**, 27, **49**, **58**
Penny Black **10**, 12, **44**, 76
Penny Red 12, **22**, **23**, 23
Perforations **23**, 37, **43**, **55**, **66**, **67**, 67, 71, **75**, 88, 89, 90, 91, **92**
Photogravure 17, **36**, **38**, **39**, 39, 89, 90, 91
PHQ cards: see Maximum Cards
Pigeon post **61**
Plate number **22**, 90
Pneumatic post 60, **61**
Poland **62**
Pony Express (U.S.A.) **20**
Portugal **78**
Postage Due stamps **33**, **35**, **38**, 90
Postal history 8–9, 90: see also Covers

Postal stationery 44, 90
Post horn 8, **9**
Postmarks **23**, 23, **45**, 50, **78**, **79**, 79, 88, 89
Post Office **7**, 8, **9**, 10, **23**, 40, 44, **46**, 47, 79
"Post Office" Mauritius stamps **56**
Presentation Packs 40, 90

Railways: see Thematics: Trains
Recess printing **38**, **39**, 39, 76, 89, 90, 91: See also Engraved stamps
Red Cross **64**, 64, 81, 92
Roosevelt, Franklin (U.S. President) **29**
Russia **11**, **18**, 30, **31**, **42**, 43, **45**, 60, 62, 64, **65**, **70**, **72**, 82

St. George and the Dragon **56**
Sarawak 44, **45**, 83
Schafer, Albert **12**, 12
Ships: see Thematics: Ships
Sierra Leone (Africa) **40**, 43
Singapore **43**, **72**
Soaking off stamps 44, **50**, **51**, 91
South Africa **36**, **56**, **81**, 83
Souvenir sheets **40**, 40, 91: see also Miniature sheets
Space: see Thematics: Space
Spain **8**, **11**, 17, 20, **21**, 24, **28**, 30, **33**, **43**, 43, **73**, 76
Special Delivery **35**, 35
Sperati, Juan de 47: see also Forgery
Sport: see Thematics: Sport
Sri Lanka 33, 83: see also Ceylon
Stamp dealers **12**, 12, 14, **48**, 49, 50, 53
Stamp murder **26**, 26, 27, **57**
Stamp-on-stamp: see Thematics: Stamp-on-stamp
Stamp printing **36–39**, 36–39, 57, 88, 89, 90, 91: see also Gravure; Intaglio; Letterpress;

Lithography; Offset lithography; Photogravure; Recess printing; Surface printing: Typography
Stamp shops 14, **48**, **49**, 49, 50
Statue of Liberty **14**, **25**
Stencils **71**
Stockbooks **48**, 69
Straits Settlements (Malaysia) 44, 83
Surface printing: see Letterpress
Sweden **25**, **41**, **45**, 76, **78**
Switzerland **9**, 30,47, **53**, 57, **78**

"Talking stamps" (Bhutan) **42**
Tangier 33
Tête bêche 57, 91
Thematic collecting 6, **7**, **16**, **17**, 17, **18**, **19**, 19, 73
Thematics
  Aircraft 17, **18**, **34**, **57**, **58**, **59**, 73
  Animals 6, **14**, **17**, **18**, 19, **20**, **21**, **25**, **31**, **34**, **35**, **41**, **52**, **54**, 61, **72**, 73, **77**, **78**, **81**
  Automobiles **18**
  Bicycles **7**, **18**, **56**
  Boy Scouts **17**, **56**
  Butterflies **6**, 17, **36**
  Dinosaurs **17**
  Disney **16**
  Flowers and trees 3, **17**, 19, **38**, **39**, **47**
  Music 19, **25**, 74, 76
  Railways: see Trains
  Ships **4**, **9**, 17, **18**, **19**, 19, **24**, **33**, **39**, 60, **62**, 63
  Space **16**, **42**, **72**
  Sport **17**, **21**, 24, **37**, 54, **73**, **80**
  Stamp-on-stamp **11**, **56**, 57
  Trains 14, 17, **18**, **20**, 35, **48**
  Transportation **8**, **9**, **15**, 16, **18**, **19**, 19, **20**, **25**, **30**, **32**, **34**, **35**, **45**, **56**, **57**, **58**, **59**, **60**, **61**, **62**, **63**, **72**
Three-dimensional stamps **43**
Tibet 33
Tin Can Mail **60**
Tonga **42**, **60**

Trains: see Thematics: Trains
Transportation: see Thematics: Transportation
Twopenny Blue 12
Typography: see Letterpress

United Nations **54**
United States **4**, **7**, **10**, **14**, 14, **17**, **19**, **20**, **22**, **25**, **26**, 27, **29**, **32**, 33, **34**, **35**, **37**, **46**, **53**, **54**, **57**, **58**, **59**, **62**, **63**, 64, **65**, **68**, **72**, **73**, **74**, 74, **78**, **79**, 79, **80**, 80, 82
U.N.: see United Nations
U.S., U.S.A.: see United States
U.S.S.R.: see Russia

Varieties **7**, **54**, **67**, **74**: see also Errors
Verne, Jules **16**, 20, **77**
Victoria, Queen **10**, 10, **23**

Washington, George **10**
Watermark, 54, **55**, **66**, **67**, 67, 74, 91
Wells Fargo (U.S.A.) **20**
West Berlin **14**, 81: see also Germany
West Germany **5**, **14**, **16**, **18**, **64**, 82: see also Germany
Whiting, Charles **10**
World Cup (soccer) **24**

Year of the Child **73**
Yugoslavia 30, 82

Zeppelin airships 44, **59**, **74**
Zip code 7